This book feels like sitting down with a wise, longtime friend who has walked the path and is now lighting the way for others. Shanti Kaur weaves decades of experience into guidance that is both spiritually resonant and refreshingly honest. It's not just about doing a practice—it's about becoming more yourself in the process.

— DEV SUROOP KAUR, VOCAL EMPOWERMENT
MENTOR & MUSICIAN

The Path of Sadhana is an incredible tool for anyone from any walk of life looking to begin or even deepen their own personal spiritual journey. It is filled with a lifetime of personal practice and stories, and hits all the key components of a daily sadhana. Fantastic work.

— JUGAT GURU SINGH KHALSA, TEACHER AND
SPIRITUAL LIFE COACH

This marvelous book contains what I call actionable wisdom. It is not solely words to absorb. It has practical advice for when you're stuck, when the mind rebels, and other impediments to being able to live in higher consciousness. Pick any chapter and you will find techniques that are practical and uplifting. Shanti shares her lived experiences with so much compassion. Enjoy!

— HARGOPAL KAUR, TEACHER AND HEALER

THE
PATH
of
SADHANA

THE PATH OF SADHANA

A PRACTICAL GUIDE TO DAILY MEDITATION

HOW TO BUILD A CONSISTENT PRACTICE TO CULTIVATE SELF-MASTERY AND SPIRITUAL GROWTH

SHANTI KAUR KHALSA

COPYRIGHT

CONTENTS

*This book is dedicated with love and great appreciation to the women of
the Khalsa.*
Daughters of the Khalsa, in your strength, our future lies.
– Song of the Khalsa by Livtar Singh Khalsa

ਕੀਤਾ ਲੋੜੀਐ ਕੰਮੁ ਸੁ ਹਰਿ ਪਹਿ ਆਖੀਐ ॥
ਕਾਰਜੁ ਦੇਇ ਸਵਾਰਿ ਸਤਿਗੁਰ ਸਚੁ ਸਾਖੀਐ ॥

Whatever work you wish to accomplish,

Tell it to the Lord.

He will resolve your affairs,

The True Guru gives His guarantee of Truth.

— GURU NANAK DEV JI

INTRODUCTION

I began attending morning sadhana in my early college years at the local 3HO[i] ashram. Every morning before dawn, we would gather in the sadhana room for meditation. Wrapped in my shawl, surrounded by the gentle hush of early morning, my life began to change. There was no grand revelation—just a quiet sense of arriving, as if a door had opened to a part of me I hadn't yet met. In that shared experience, the noise of my mind grew faint, and I caught my first glimpse of the steady silence that lives beneath it all. This was the beginning of my journey into sadhana, a daily rhythm that would come to shape me from the inside out. A practice that would transform my life in ways I never imagined.

Sadhana, the commitment to a daily spiritual practice, is not tied to any religion or dogma. At its core, it is a holistic daily routine that weaves together the threads of spiritual disciplines, including prayer, *pranayama* (yogic breathing), yoga, and meditation. It is a path that invites us to connect with our inner selves, to find balance amidst the chaos, and to open our hearts to each moment.

This book serves as your guide to establishing and maintaining a personalized daily sadhana. Whether you're a beginner taking your first steps or an experienced meditator looking to deepen your journey, this book is for you. Although I am a Sikh, sadhana is a practice that applies to all faiths. I hope to offer you a roadmap, a series of steps to guide you toward a successful daily sadhana.

Allow me to share a bit about myself. My name is Shanti Kaur, and I have been practicing meditation within the Sikh tradition for over 50 years. I had the privilege of studying directly under Yogi Bhajan for more than three decades. Today, I continue this path as a meditation teacher and writer.

As you journey through this book, you'll find a structure designed to support you. We'll explore setting up a dedicated meditation space, choosing the right time for practice, and selecting the length of time that suits your life. You'll find guidance on overcoming common challenges like motivation, fatigue, and mental clutter. Detailed instructions on breathing techniques, yoga sets, and chanting await you in the appendix, based on Kundalini Yoga as taught by Yogi Bhajan®.

There are many myths surrounding the practice of sadhana. Some believe it is too complex or restricted to certain spiritual traditions. In truth, sadhana is adaptable and accessible to everyone. It is a practice that welcomes you as you are, offering you tools to enrich your spiritual path, whatever that path may be. Inclusivity is at the heart of this book. There are tailored options for various religious traditions, ensuring that sadhana can complement and enrich any spiritual journey. The universal appeal of sadhana lies in its simplicity and its profound ability to transform our lives.

Maintaining a daily sadhana has many benefits. Scientifically and personally, it has been demonstrated to enhance mental well-being, promote spiritual growth, and develop self-mastery. As you integrate sadhana into your life, you may find yourself more centered, more connected, and more alive.

As you step onto this path, may you do so with a sense of commitment and wonder. The journey of sadhana holds the power to reshape your inner landscape in quiet, transformative ways. It is a doorway to a fuller, more awakened life. Welcome to sadhana! May it bring peace in your heart, strength in your spirit, and awareness in every step.

1

LAYING THE FOUNDATION OF A DAILY SADHANA

H ave you ever woken up in the stillness of dawn, feeling the world's embrace before its daily rush? It is a moment where time seems to pause, offering a space of clarity and peace. This quiet hour presents a profound opportunity for transformation, treasured by all spiritual paths for its divine stillness and the promise of a clear mind. As the sun rises every day, so too can you, nurtured by a practice that integrates body, mind, and spirit. Over the years, sadhana has been my anchor, a daily practice that has grounded me and opened my heart to life's possibilities. Through this chapter, I invite you to explore the roots of this transformative tradition, to gain a deeper understanding of its full breadth and depth.

UNDERSTANDING SADHANA – BEYOND MEDITATION

The etymology of the word *sadhana* is found in classical Sanskrit and is deeply rooted in Asia's spiritual and philosophical traditions. The root word, "sadh," means "to accomplish" in Sanskrit, and in the Sikh tradition, it refers to being "spiritually accomplished." Sadhana describes personal effort that is intentional, dedicated, and sustained towards one's spiritual elevation. While the word originates in India, sadhana can be applied to all spiritual traditions. One who has a consistent sadhana practice is known, with great respect, as a *sadhak*.

Sadhana is a tapestry of daily routine that weaves through your lifestyle, whether you're just beginning or have been meditating for years. At its heart, sadhana is about sustained spiritual growth through consistent practice. It is not limited to any particular faith but harmonizes with all spiritual orientations. This openness is what makes sadhana a universal practice of discipline and commitment. Engaging with sadhana means embracing a holistic approach that honors your entire being.

The multifaceted nature of sadhana encompasses physical, mental, and spiritual dimensions. **Physical practices** like yoga and pranayama help prepare your body, creating a vessel capable of sustaining more profound meditation. **Mantra and meditation** expand the mind, enhancing concentration and creativity. **Spiritual reflections** and prayers nurture your spirit, offering moments of introspection and connection to something greater.

We do sadhana to connect with the deeper currents of our being and to remember who we truly are beyond the world's noise. It is a conscious act of turning inward, creating space each day to listen, breathe, and align with something greater than us. Through regular practice, sadhana becomes a sacred time to nourish the soul, refine the mind, and walk gently toward the Divine within. It is a personal and self-directed routine that allows you to incorporate cultural and religious elements meaningful to you. Sadhana is a lifelong endeavor—there's no destination, just a continual unfolding process where each day brings new insights.

The benefits of maintaining a consistent sadhana are profound. You'll experience enhanced self-awareness and introspection, opening new horizons and strengthening your connection to personal beliefs. It helps cultivate personal freedom and fearlessness by reducing stress and anxiety. By working to mitigate the impact of anger on your mental and physical well-being, sadhana opens you up to giving and receiving love.

As you embark on this exploration of sadhana, remember it is not a magic potion but an invitation to deepen your understanding of yourself and the world around you. It takes work. Your commitment is to a practice and a way of living that honors the Sacred in every moment. Your journey with sadhana will be as unique as you are, offering endless opportunities for growth and discovery.

Historical and Cultural Roots of Sadhana

ਤਾਤ ਮਾਤ ਗੁਰ ਅਲਖ ਅਰਾਧਾ ॥
ਬਹੁ ਬਿਧਿ ਜੋਗ ਸਾਧਨਾ ਸਾਧਾ ॥3॥

My parents practiced meditation, sadhana, and yoga
for union with the Incomprehensible Lord 3.

Guru Gobind Singh, the 10th Sikh Guru, writes in the Bachitra
Natik in the 17th century.

Sadhana traces its roots back to ancient Indian traditions, where it evolved as a spiritual practice aimed at achieving enlightenment. Ancient texts describe it as a means of connecting with the Divine, a process that integrates the body and mind. With time, sadhana evolved and was influenced by spiritual teachings and religious philosophies.

In Sikhism, the tradition I have followed for the past 50 years, it is a core practice for devotees to rise early and meditate during the *Amrit Vela*, "the ambrosial hours." This time, before the sun rises, is considered ideal for meditation. Meditating in the early morning is deeply woven into the Sikh way of life.

Across different societies, sadhana has been both adopted and adapted. It has found its place as an ancient practice with contemporary appeal in Western and Eastern spiritual traditions. Amrit Vela in Sikhism exemplifies this, where practitioners wake in the tranquil hours before dawn to recite prayers, meditate, and listen to *kirtan*—a form of devotional music. Similarly, Hindu and Buddhist temples are alive with people and chanting before dawn. Some of my sweetest memories are meditating in Buddhist temples in Japan, Tibet, and Bhutan during the pre-dawn hours.

And in the West, the echo of sadhana can be found in Christian devotional practices, which are prevalent in monasteries and convents worldwide. A beautiful experience is to join the Franciscan monks in the early hours at the tomb of Saint Francis in the Basilica of Saint Francis of Assisi, Italy, to recite prayers. In the Jewish tradition, *Shacharit* is recited after dawn, offering gratitude and aligning oneself with the Divine Will. In Islam, the *Fajr* is the first of five daily prayers and is performed just before sunrise. It consists of 2 *rak'ahs* (units of prayer) with a special emphasis on reflection. This early morning prayer is a great blessing, filled with Divine energy. The Prophet Muhammad said: "*The two rak'ahs of Fajr are better than the world and all it contains*" (as recorded in the *Sahih Muslim*). Devotion in the early hours before dawn is a common element among all the major religions, illustrating how the concept of sadhana, though not necessarily referred to by the same name, connects various spiritual traditions.

Beyond being a personal meditative practice, sadhana is a foundation for community and spiritual unity. Rituals associated with early morning meditation hold deep significance, enhancing collective identities and fostering a sense of belonging. For instance, in Sikh communities, meditation during the Amrit Vela creates bonds that strengthen community ties. Such gatherings transcend individual meditation, becoming collective experiences that unite participants in shared spiritual goals. Sadhana nurtures personal growth and reinforces cultural and religious identities within communities through this communal aspect.

Dispelling Misconceptions about Sadhana

Sadhana transcends religious boundaries, offering a spiritual path adaptable to any faith or belief system. It invites everyone to explore its benefits regardless of their spiritual background. It is a misconception that sadhana requires a life of isolation. Sadhana integrates seamlessly into daily life, whether you're in a bustling city or the quiet countryside. It doesn't necessitate withdrawing from the world but instead enriches your interaction with it.

Householders often feel they're excluded from deep spiritual practice, thinking that this is only for those who renounce worldly life and dedicate themselves to a spiritual journey in a cave or mountain retreat. Actually, sadhana is uniquely suited for those living amidst daily responsibilities. It provides a framework for spiritual growth within the parameters of everyday life, allowing householders to achieve profound spiritual focus. The flexibility of sadhana accommodates the varied rhythms of a busy life, proving that spiritual expansion is achievable and enhanced by the challenges and joys of family and work.

> *The technology of sadhana, as given by Guru Nanak, was not intended for those who are hermits or those who leave the world for the top of a mountain. It was a technology meant clearly, and laid down clearly, for those who want to live as householders and continue the process of life, for those who want to live as soldiers and continue the battle against negativity, and those saintly people who can elevate themselves while living on this planet Earth. Yogi Bhajan, 2/6/1977*

The perception that sadhana is complex deters many from exploring its potential. In reality, it can be as simple as starting with a few moments of focused breathing or a simple meditation. Sadhana meets you where you are, allowing for gradual progression in complexity as you become more comfortable. There's no need to commit to elaborate rituals immediately; simplicity is the key to consistency. Begin with basic practices, and as you grow more confident, you can add additional elements that resonate with your journey.

Time commitment is another common concern. Many worry they don't have enough time for sadhana. But the strength of your sadhana lies in its adaptability. Quality is emphasized over quantity, whether you have five minutes or two hours. A focused 15-minute meditation can be more beneficial than an unfocused hour. It's about setting a time commitment you can sustain, even on the busiest days. Consistency, not duration, is what nurtures growth and transformation.

Sadhana's accessibility lies in its ability to integrate into daily life without overwhelming it. It's not about isolating yourself from the world but finding peace within it. We open the door to a profound and approachable practice by debunking these myths and misconceptions. Sadhana invites you to explore its depths at your own pace, bringing spirituality into your everyday life.

THE ESSENCE OF DAILY SPIRITUAL PRACTICE

Sadhana is an invitation to embark on a path toward spiritual development and inner peace. It is a practice that calls us to transform from within, shedding self-denigrating habits that no longer serve us, and embracing personal growth and transformation. For many, it's about connecting with the Divine or our higher selves, a connection that offers solace and guidance through life's uncertainties. Imagine the freedom of living without the chains of negative self-talk and the grace that follows when we align our intentions with our actions. This freedom is the promise of sadhana—where personal transformation is not just possible but inevitable.

Intention is the compass that guides your spiritual practice. With clear intentions, each day of sadhana becomes a step toward fulfilling our spiritual aspirations. When we focus our thoughts and actions on our spiritual goals, we find alignment between our daily lives and our deeper purpose. Setting intentions might start with something as broad as a desire for peace or compassion, for ourselves or others. Over time, these intentions become more specific, evolving into powerful affirmations that shape our reality. As we grow with our sadhana, our intentions become more and more important on our spiritual path.

Consistency in sadhana leads to profound spiritual growth, much like a drop of water can eventually shape a stone. Each day we do our sadhana, we build resilience and patience, qualities that help us navigate life's challenges with grace and strength. Overcoming challenges becomes part of the process, not something to fear but to embrace. In these moments of struggle, we discover our capacity for expansion.

With sadhana, there is no final achievement to strive for. It is all about the journey. The Chinese philosopher Lao Tzu classically said,

A good traveler has no fixed plans and is not intent on arriving.

This speaks directly about our sadhana. It is a practice that evolves with us, shaping new pathways as we move through life. Our journey with sadhana is ever-unfolding, revealing deeper layers of understanding and connection. As we commit to daily practice, we become more attuned to the subtle shifts within ourselves and around us. This awareness allows us to navigate life with greater ease and sensitivity, opening us to the beauty of each moment and the infinite potential within us.

The path of sadhana is one of continual transformation, where each step brings us closer to our center. It is a practice that invites us to explore the depths of our being, to find peace in the present moment, and to live with intention and purpose.

Building a Personalized Sadhana Framework

When I first started a sadhana practice, I lived in the Guru Ram Das Ashram, a 3HO community in New Hampshire. I was attending college and was a young and devoted seeker of the Divine. We practiced sadhana as a group, with each person in the ashram rising at 3:30 AM to arrive in the sadhana room by 4:00 AM. We did the 2 ½-hour sadhana as taught by Yogi Bhajan, which included prayer, yoga, and chanting. I loved it and waited all day until I could sleep, get up, and do it again. Group sadhana in 3HO ashrams continues today, known as the *Aquarian Sadhana*, and forms the basis of community life. Many ashrams live-stream their morning sadhana, making it available to anyone who wishes to join.

While group sadhana is a fantastic and foundational experience, it may not be available to you, impractical, or not suited to your phase of life. Creating a sadhana practice then becomes a personal endeavor that reflects your unique spiritual needs and aspirations. It begins with assessing what you truly seek from this practice. Think about what spiritual nourishment you crave—perhaps greater self-mastery or a deeper connection to the universe. Consider how much time you can genuinely commit. Maybe it's 15 minutes in the morning or an hour on weekends. Perhaps it is longer. Your practice should be sustainable, not a burden that adds pressure to your life.

To build your framework, start each session with an invocation for guidance. This can be a simple moment of silence or a prayer inviting wisdom and clarity. Next comes *pranayama*, or breathing techniques, which calm the mind and set the stage for meditation. Follow this with yoga or gentle stretching to release tension, ensuring your body is comfortable for sitting meditation. Mantra chanting or a Kundalini Yoga kriya is the central element that focuses the mind and elevates the spirit. Close your practice with a prayer of gratitude, acknowledging the time you've spent nurturing your soul. Feel free to adapt this framework to your religious tradition.

I encourage flexibility in your practice. Life is unpredictable, and sadhana should adapt to its ebbs and flows. Experiment with various meditation techniques until you find one that resonates with you. Adjust your practice accordingly as circumstances change, such as taking on new jobs or assuming family responsibilities. The key is maintaining your commitment to daily meditation, no matter how your routine evolves.

In crafting a sadhana that's uniquely yours, remember that this practice is both dynamic and forgiving. It's not about following strict rules but discovering what fills you with peace and purpose. Your sadhana should reflect who you are and who you aspire to become. As you explore this path, embrace the insights and growth that emerge from each session. In nurturing this sacred space within yourself, you cultivate wisdom that touches every aspect of your life.

Building a sadhana practice that resonates with you creates a foundation for profound and enduring spiritual growth. The journey may be yours alone, but its impact will ripple through all areas of your existence, bringing balance, clarity, and joy.

2

CREATING YOUR
MEDITATION SPACE

The world abounds with beautiful temples and sacred spaces dedicated to the Divine. Perhaps you are one of the lucky ones who regularly access these fantastic places for daily meditation. But for the rest of us, let's explore how to create a sacred space at home.

Of course, the best solution is to have a dedicated meditation pavilion that you can craft into an inspiring sadhana space. A close second is a dedicated sadhana room in your home, where you can infuse the vibration of meditation and prayer, creating a sanctuary that envelops you the moment you enter. In a sadhana room, it is best to have no other activities conducted there, preserving the atmosphere of sacredness and peace.

The author meditating at the beautiful Sri Harimandir Sahib in Amritsar, India.

While these options are excellent, they are a rare luxury. When I first began practicing sadhana at home, we lived in a small space with a newborn. There was not even a spare corner to sit on the floor! So, I made do on the couch with a portable "sadhana kit" that I kept in a lovely satchel, and I kept my chanting to a whisper to not wake the family. Today, I have a sweet meditation area on one side of my home office. Gracefully laid out with a beautiful altar, scriptures, and meaningful items, it is my "go-to" place at any time of day. I thought that perhaps the vibration of the computer and pull of pending work would interfere with my concentration, but honestly, it doesn't. It works for me, and it can work for you.

DESIGNING A SADHANA SPACE AT HOME

Your sadhana space doesn't have to be elaborate, it simply needs to be a place that invites stillness and consciousness. Whether it's a dedicated room or a quiet corner, the key is to find a space where interruptions are minimal. If a dedicated room is unavailable, the corner of a multipurpose room, a cozy alcove, or even a mobile kit with essentials in a small bag can work beautifully.

Personalizing your space makes it sacred. Incorporate items that resonate deeply with your spiritual journey—perhaps a photo, an heirloom, or a stone from a meaningful place. Choose colors that soothe or energize you. Whether earthy or vibrant, these choices should reflect your soul and intentions. Your sacred space is an extension of your spirit. It should welcome you as you are, creating a boundary between the mundane and the divine—a place where your inner world can open freely.

Essentials of a Sadhana Space

Start with comfortable seating: a cushion, chair, or bench that allows you to sit in stillness without strain. Proper seating can make all the difference, transforming discomfort into ease.

A focal point, such as a small altar, helps anchor your attention with a sculpture, a candle, or a special object that reminds you why you've come to sit.

Bring in elements of nature, such as a plant, a flower, or a smooth stone. Natural materials, such as wood or natural fibers, help connect your space to the earth and instill a sense of calm.

Organize your tools so they're easily accessible, such as a shawl, cushion, incense, or journal. This keeps your sadhana space ready and inviting. Simplicity is essential. Clutter distracts, so keep only what supports your practice.

Cultural or spiritual symbols deepen the sacredness of your meditation space. Statues, images of divine beings, or sacred texts offer a tangible link to your beliefs and aspirations. A mandala, yantra, or a piece of jewelry passed through generations can ground your practice in lineage and memory.

The altar in my meditation corner.

Souvenirs from spiritual journeys, such as a prayer flag or a memento from a sacred site, bring a sense of pilgrimage into your home. These are not just decorations; they're reminders of growth, moments of clarity, or transformations you've experienced.

Art can be a powerful ally. A painting that evokes peace or a photo of nature can serve as a silent companion, gently inspiring your inner work. Select images or objects that uplift and center you.

Lighting transforms a space from ordinary to sacred. Dim, warm light creates a cocoon of stillness, helping to ease the transition from your daily mindset into meditation. The flicker of candlelight can symbolize the spark of inner awareness, and the light of a flame in the darkness draws your mental focus like nothing else.

Scent also plays a central role. Natural incense, such as sandalwood or agarwood, or essential oils, like frankincense, jasmine, or sage, help clear the mind and bring clarity. These aromas can mark the beginning of your practice, signaling your body and mind to relax.

Sound is the final element. Whether it's a singing bowl, soft chants, or the natural rhythm of silence, it should support rather than intrude. What matters is that the space sounds like stillness to you.

Choosing and Arranging Meditation Tools

Creating a great meditation space involves selecting the right tools to enhance your practice.

Mala beads are a valuable aid. Their smooth texture slips through your fingers as you count each breath or mantra. They add rhythm to your meditation, grounding you in the present. If you're more digitally inclined, consider using a timer app on your phone. It allows you to set a specific duration without the distraction of checking the clock. This way, you can immerse yourself fully, knowing your session will end at the right time.

Pranayama apps can be a great addition, especially when incorporating breathing exercises into your practice. These apps offer guided sessions that help you explore various breathing techniques at your own pace. As you follow along, you'll notice how the breath can transform your mind, bringing calm and clarity. It's like having a personal coach guiding you through each breath.

Arranging these tools within your meditation space should be intentional yet intuitive. Keep your cushion or bench ready, inviting you to settle down whenever the mood strikes. Place your mala beads within easy reach, such as on a small table or shelf, so they're readily available when needed. Your phone or device for pranayama apps and timers should be easily accessible but not intrusive. (Remember to set your phone to silent mode to avoid disturbances.) For music, create a playlist that aligns with your intentions for each session, whether you're seeking relaxation, focus, or inspiration.

Incorporating these elements into your practice doesn't have to be complicated. It's about finding what works for you and creating the right space. Remember that there is no one-size-fits-all approach; it's about personalizing your meditation environment to suit your needs and preferences. As you experiment with different tools and arrangements, you'll discover what enhances your practice and brings you closer to that coveted state of inner silence.

By thoughtfully choosing and arranging these tools, you're not just decorating a space, you're creating an experience that invites you into the present moment and encourages exploration of your inner landscape. This arrangement will evolve as you do, adapting to reflect the growth and change in your practice.

WHEN A DEDICATED SPACE IS NOT AN OPTION

You may not have the luxury of a permanent meditation spot, especially when starting your sadhana practice. In such cases, a mobile sadhana bag becomes invaluable. Pack essentials like a cushion, a shawl, a small altar piece, and your favorite incense into a satchel. This makes it easy to create your sacred space wherever you find yourself. The unpacking and setting up can become a ritual, signaling the transition from daily life to spiritual practice.

One of the advantages of a sadhana bag is that it can accompany you outside. When the weather is warm, meditating outside is a wonderful experience. In the cool, quiet hours before the sun rises, it is a delight to expand your mind into the vastness of nature, with all its sounds and scents. A beautiful meditation is to lie on your back and look up into the stars, projecting your consciousness into the immensity of space.

To wrap up this chapter, remember that your meditation space should reflect who you are and what you need. It's about creating an environment that draws you in, keeps you there, and makes every session meaningful. With your meditation space thoughtfully crafted, you're set to explore further dimensions of your practice.

3
ESTABLISHING A CONSISTENT TIME FOR YOUR SADHANA

Meditation is good at any time of day. However, when developing a sadhana practice, it is beneficial to start meditating at a consistent time and allow it to become part of your life. Let it change as your life changes, but have the intention of consistency. Half the battle of a daily sadhana is just sitting down to do it! Having a regular sadhana time becomes part of your routine, removing the decision-making from the equation.

SELECTING THE OPTIMAL TIME FOR DAILY PRACTICE

The time you choose to meditate can have a profound influence on your experience. Choosing the right time to meditate isn't just about fitting it into your schedule; it's about aligning your meditation time with the natural rhythms of your life, which enhances your practice. For Sikhs, meditating in the Amrit Vela, the early morning hours before sunrise, is an integral part of our spiritual discipline. Early morning sessions, before the demands of the day encroach, offer a serene space for reflection and focus. It's like tapping into an untouched reservoir of peace that sets a positive tone for everything that follows.

If you're not up for a pre-dawn start, consider how evening sessions can benefit your life. As the day winds down, meditation allows you to unwind and reflect on the events of the day. This practice can help transform tension into relaxation, facilitating a smooth transition into restful sleep. Experimenting with different times can help you find your sweet spot—a time when meditation feels most natural and rewarding. This time must also be in sync with your environment, not when your presence is demanded elsewhere.

Allowing your meditation schedule to be flexible can be important in maintaining consistency amidst life's chaos. Life is unpredictable, and rigidity often leads to frustration. Allow for varied session lengths to accommodate busy days or unexpected events. Incorporate buffer times into your schedule to ease transitions between activities without rushing. A weekly planner can be invaluable for penciling in meditation slots, allowing you to visualize your commitment.

Sometimes, no matter how hard you try, it just doesn't work out. You have to be okay with that; let it go and start again tomorrow.

Benefits of Meditating in the Amrit Vela

ਅੰਮ੍ਰਿਤ ਵੇਲਾ ਸਚੁ ਨਾਉ ਵਡਿਆਈ ਵੀਚਾਰੁ ॥
ਕਰਮੀ ਆਵੈ ਕਪੜਾ ਨਦਰੀ ਮੋਖੁ ਦੁਆਰੁ ॥
ਨਾਨਕ ਏਵੈ ਜਾਣੀਐ ਸਭੁ ਆਪੇ ਸਚਿਆਰੁ ॥੪॥

In the Amrit Vela, chant the True Name, and contemplate His Greatness.
By the karma of past actions, the robe of your physical body is obtained.
By His Grace, the Gate of Liberation is found.
O Nanak, know this well: the True One Himself is All. ||4||
Guru Nanak Dev Ji, Japji Sahib

In the quiet hours before dawn, a magical stillness envelopes the world. This is a time of pure potential, where the air holds a promise of clarity and calm. This serene window of time is revered for meditation. It's believed that before the sun floods the earth with light, the vibrations of life are at their calmest, allowing for a profound connection to inner silence. Early morning meditation doesn't just clear the mind; it fills you with clarity and purpose, preparing you to meet the day with a centered heart.

The absence of worldly noise allows for an uninterrupted dialogue with your inner self, a conversation that often gets drowned out as the day progresses. The silence is not just external, but also internal, providing fertile ground for spiritual growth.

Transitioning your schedule into a new routine requires patience. Your body needs time to adapt to earlier nights and mornings. Ensuring you get enough sleep is crucial, so aim for seven or eight hours to avoid burnout. As your practice matures, you may discover that your body requires less sleep, a testament to the rejuvenating power of meditation in the early morning. Letting your body adjust gradually makes this change sustainable and gratifying, so start slowly and progressively push the time earlier for morning sadhana. Giving up is easy, but staying committed reaps rewards beyond measure.

As life ebbs and flows, maintain flexibility in your meditation schedule. Life's unpredictability demands adaptability, whether adjusting session lengths or changing times. Regularly revisiting and revising your schedule ensures it remains effective and aligns with your evolving life circumstances.

It Can Be Hard to Get Up in the Early Morning!

It felt like an uphill battle when I first started waking up for meditation. Rising early in the morning can be a daunting task. The warmth of the bed, the comfort of those last few minutes of sleep is all so tempting! But there's a magic in those dark hours that makes the struggle worthwhile. The world whispers, "Wake up and find your peace before the day begins." I recall the initial resistance and the internal dialogue that sometimes convinced me to stay under the covers. Yet, each morning that I chose to get up, I found a little more clarity, a little more peace. Establishing this routine gradually transforms it from a chore into a cherished ritual. The beauty of it lies in its quiet predictability; the world may rush and roar, but your mornings remain a sanctuary.

Guru Nanak said it clearly - Rise early before the sun. Only a fool rises after the sun! Wake up early so you can have your own time, your own personality, your own technology, and prepare yourself to face the neurosis of the day. Yogi Bhajan, 1/6/1977

In my early days of practicing sadhana, the alarm clock was both friend and foe. I relied on it to pull me from sleep's embrace, yet dreaded its piercing, nagging call. Over time, as my routine solidified, my body began to anticipate the alarm, stirring me awake moments before it sounded.

If you share your life with a partner, a ringing alarm in the very early morning may not be a viable option. I have found that a fitness watch can be a helpful alternative, vibrating softly on your wrist to rouse you without disturbing your partner's sleep. There are elaborate and expensive fitness watches, which are great but unnecessary. Some very affordable models work just fine as alarm clocks.

Your body needs time to adjust to this new rhythm, but you may find your sleep shifts as you become more experienced with your practice. You may wake refreshed after less sleep than usual—a curious blessing of regular meditation.

HOW LONG SHOULD I MEDITATE?

There is no single rule for how long you "should" meditate, because meditation is a profoundly personal journey. However, specific time frames can offer guidance depending on your intention and experience level. Even 15 minutes daily can yield noticeable benefits for beginners, including reduced stress, improved focus, and a subtle shift toward greater calm. Perhaps your entire sadhana consists of breathing techniques aimed at achieving mind-body balance. The key is not how long you sit, but how consistently you return.

As your practice deepens, you may find that 20 to 30 minutes of daily meditation offers a sweet spot—enough time to move past surface-level thoughts and enter a quieter, more introspective space within. Many traditions, including those in mindfulness and yogic lineages, recommend 20–30 minutes as a foundational daily practice. In Kundalini Yoga and similar paths, specific meditations are practiced for 11, 22, or 31 minutes, based on energetic effects observed through tradition and experience. Combine that with devotional prayer, some pranayama, and a little yoga, and before you know it, you'll have spent a wonderful hour in sadhana.

More extended periods may be more suitable for experienced sadhaks. Early morning meditations often extend to 62 minutes or even 2.5 hours, considered powerful durations for rewiring mental patterns, clearing karma, and cultivating deep stillness. But this level of commitment comes gradually, often through devotion rather than discipline alone.

At 3HO Ashrams worldwide, Aquarian Sadhana is practiced as a group and lasts approximately 2.5 hours. This is not a random number. Sikhs believe in the concept of *dasvand*, which involves donating 10% of our energy and resources for the greater good. 10% of 24 hours is about 2.5 hours, which is the dasvand of our time. Sadhana begins at 4:00 AM with the Sikh prayer, *Japji Sahib*, followed by 30 minutes of yoga and an hour of chanting. By 6:30 AM, sadhana is concluded, and everyone is off to start their day.

The commitment to long meditations can be found in all spiritual traditions. During a recent trip to Kongobuji Temple, the head temple of the Shingon Esoteric Buddhist sect at Mt. Koya in Japan, my host explained that all monks complete at least one 100-day meditation intensive in their lifetime, and many undertake multiple retreats. The monk enters a meditation hut and has no contact with anyone until his 100 days are complete. Food and water are brought and left by the door for the sadhak to retrieve in total privacy.

Meditation hut at the Kongobuji Temple where a monk will complete a 100-day meditation.

Ultimately, you will find that there is ALWAYS more that you can do, and this will continue to draw you beguilingly onward. Remember, this is a lifelong practice, and there is no rush. The right length of time for you is the one that brings you fully present, not rushed, not strained, but sincerely engaged. Let your duration reflect your relationship with the practice: reverent, consistent, and alive. Even a brief meditation practiced with full concentration is far more transformative than a longer one performed out of obligation or filled with distraction.

Livtar Singh Khalsa wisely wrote in his song, "Beyond the Far Horizon,"

> There's a reason the world is round, new horizons around every bend. So, we know that no matter how far we go, we can never reach the end. There is no end.

Start where you are. Build gently. Let time on the cushion be time with your soul.

Crafting a Flexible Meditation Schedule

Of course, the Amrit Vela isn't the only time you can practice your sadhana. Life can be unpredictable, and maintaining a rigid meditation schedule at any time of day is often unrealistic. Embracing flexibility in your practice enables you to adapt to life's ebbs and flows without losing focus. Consider adjusting the length of your meditation sessions to match your daily schedule. Some days may allow a full hour, while others offer only ten minutes. This adaptable approach keeps your practice alive, allowing it to grow and shift with your ever-changing life circumstances.

Building a customizable schedule is about finding harmony between daily responsibilities and meditation. Anchoring meditation to daily activities, such as pairing it right after your morning tea or scheduling it just before bed, can make it a seamless part of your day. This integration reduces resistance, as meditation becomes naturally woven into your life rather than an isolated task. Over time, these anchored moments become cherished rituals, grounding you amidst daily chaos.

Regularly reviewing and adjusting your meditation schedule and content is crucial for longevity and effectiveness. Set aside time each month to reflect on what's working and what needs tweaking. Life stages bring personal and professional changes, necessitating adjustments to maintain balance. This monthly reflection helps identify patterns and gaps, enabling informed adjustments that align with your current needs. Adjusting goals and expectations ensures meditation remains fulfilling rather than burdensome. A flexible approach supports sustainable growth and prevents burnout, allowing meditation to remain a source of joy and tranquility. After all, this is a lifelong endeavor.

4

CREATING AND LOVING YOUR OWN SADHANA PRACTICE

Sadhana is a daily discipline that enables the soul to align with the Divine. It may follow the timeless rhythms of traditional dharma, honoring the pathways laid by enlightened beings, or it may arise authentically from your heart's longing, shaped by your unique relationship with Spirit. Both are valid when done with devotion and consistency. Here is the flow that has worked for me, based on the Aquarian Sadhana format given by Yogi Bhajan.

As you prepare for your sadhana, begin by covering your head—a simple yet profound act of devotion. This gesture honors the sacred lineage of sadhaks who came before you, those who walked the path with steadfast love and discipline. Let it remind you that you are part of this timeless stream of devotion.

Open your practice with an invocation—an offering from your heart to the Infinite. In this moment, you invite clarity and guidance into your sacred space. It sets the tone for your journey inward, aligning you with the deeper current of your soul.

Following this, immerse yourself in pranayama, breathing techniques that center and quiet the mind. If time is short, let this be the core of your sadhana. For a more prolonged sadhana, these breathing exercises prepare the mind for further meditation, creating a foundation of calm and alertness.

Yoga and body movement are next. They awaken the body and release tension. They prepare you for sitting meditation by enhancing flexibility and strengthening your body. Picture yourself gently stretching, each movement flowing in harmony with your breath. This connection between movement and breath is where meditation begins, fostering a readiness to sit in silence without discomfort. Your body and mind are open to the transformative power of meditation.

Mantra chanting follows, where sound becomes a bridge to the divine. *Laya Yoga*, the yoga of absorption through sound, dissolves the individual mind into oneness with the Infinite through the union of sound and breath. Chanting focuses your mind and elevates your spirit, inviting profound transformation.

Conclude your practice with a prayer of gratitude. Acknowledge the time spent nurturing your soul and the journey of self-discovery that unfolds within each sadhana. Gratitude amplifies the benefits of meditation, fostering a positive outlook on life and strengthening relationships. This final prayer seals your practice, leaving you with fulfillment and peace.

This is your sadhana—personal, sacred, and designed to meet your unique needs. Beyond opening and closing your practice with devotion, you can shape its flow in a way that resonates with you. You may wish to create both a "long version" and a "short version" to honor the rhythm of your days. To cultivate discipline, it is wise to plan your sequence in advance so that your practice remains steady and intentional even on the busiest mornings.

BEGIN SADHANA WITH AN INVOCATION

Begin your sadhana with an invocation—a sacred moment that aligns your heart with the Infinite. This simple act sets the tone for your practice, creating a space of reverence, clarity, and inner stillness. Whether spoken aloud or whispered within, the invocation is your soul's way of saying, *"I am here. I am ready. Guide me."* It honors the unseen forces that support your journey and opens the gateway for grace to flow into your practice. Here you can draw upon your religious tradition. All spiritual traditions are rich with prayer; this is the time to call on what you hold sacred.

In Kundalini Yoga, each session traditionally begins with the mantra, *"Ong Namo Gurudev Namo"*—a sacred link to this lineage's teachers and wisdom keepers, reaching back through generations.

Ong is the primal sound current of creativity and manifestation, a living vibration that resonates within the one chanting and throughout the surrounding environment. The sacred sound *Aum*, honored in Hinduism, Buddhism, Jainism, and other Eastern traditions, is closely related to *Ong*. While *Aum* represents the absolute and formless Divine presence, *Ong* emphasizes the dynamic, creative expression of Divine energy. Yogi Bhajan described these as two faces of the Infinite: one still, one vibrating into life.

Namo means "I humbly bow" or "I call upon with reverence."

Gurudev refers to the subtle, inner teacher that awakens through sincere spiritual practice. The etymology of the word "guru" is *gu,* meaning "darkness," and *ru,* meaning "light"; a teacher or guide that takes you from ignorance to spiritual awakening – "the one who brings you from darkness to light." In your sadhana, whether you use this mantra or another invocation sacred to your path, you connect to the timeless current of wisdom that supports and uplifts the seeker. *Ong Namo Guru Dev Namo* is a devotional and straightforward supplication for guidance.

In the Sikh tradition, the Guru is not a human teacher—it is the eternal, formless wisdom that flows directly from the Divine. This is the *Nirgun Guru*— the Guru that is beyond form, beyond attributes, beyond time. While ten human Gurus brought Sikhism to the world through their lives and teachings, Sikhs believe that the True Guru today is Infinite Consciousness, the *Naam* (the Divine Name), which manifests through the *Siri Guru Granth Sahib,* the sacred scripture of the Sikhs. When

Sikhs refer to the Guru, we are not indicating any one person or scripture; instead, we refer to the timeless Truth that dwells within the teachings, accessible through devotion, humility, and meditation. Through the grace of the Guru, the seeker is led from the illusions of the material world into the radiant experience of the Infinite.

Sikhs begin their morning sadhana with the *Japji Sahib.* Japji Sahib is the foundational prayer of the Sikhs, composed by Guru Nanak, the first Sikh Guru. It is a beautiful meditation on the nature of the Divine, the structure of creation, and the path to spiritual awakening. Recited daily by Sikhs worldwide, Japji Sahib weaves universal truths about the nature of existence and the importance of living a life of truth, humility, and remembrance of the Divine Name. Each of the 40 stanzas, known as a *pauris*, builds upon the last, guiding the seeker from the realm of duality toward union with the Divine.

I invite you to explore the Japji Sahib for yourself. You can download it for free at SikhNet.com[i], read it in poetic English in the book Peace Lagoon[ii], download the app from Sikh Dharma[iii], or listen to it in audio format from whatever platform you use – you will find it with a simple search for "Japji Sahib." It takes 10-15 minutes to recite or listen to, and it's a tradition worth cultivating.

START WITH A FEW MINUTES OF PRANAYAMA

Starting your sadhana with pranayama is like turning a key to unlock the mind's potential. Breath awareness is a simple yet profound meditation technique that centers the mind and fosters a quiet yet alert state. The breath isn't just air; it is *prana*, the lifeforce flowing through you, a bridge between the physical and the spiritual. For those mornings when time is short, let pranayama be your entire practice—even a few minutes can transform your mental space.

Pranayama offers various techniques, each with its unique rhythm and purpose. Here are just a few, and detailed instructions can be found in the appendix:

- Long Deep Breathing - fills the lungs fully and oxygenates the system.
- *Nadi Shodhana*, or alternate nostril breathing, balances the right- and left-brain hemispheres.
- 4-Part Breath - calms the nervous system and is widely used for stress relief.
- Breath of Fire - energizes and detoxifies.

These practices are more than exercises; they're gateways to improved mental clarity and reduced anxiety. They bring focus and calm, acting as anchors in the storm of daily life. The appendix contains detailed steps for each practice.

Pranayama invites you to connect with the essence of who you are, to find stillness within movement and silence within noise. Embrace this practice as part of your daily sadhana, and allow it to guide you toward greater self-mastery and inner peace. We discover profound beauty and potential through breath, transforming the ordinary into the extraordinary with each conscious inhalation and exhalation.

BASIC YOGA EXERCISES FOR MEDITATION

Yoga is excellent at any time, but here we utilize yoga as a preparation for meditation, awakening the body, calming the mind, and opening the flow of prana. Incorporating yoga into your daily sadhana creates the conditions for deeper meditation. Yoga naturally expands your capacity for sustained meditation by strengthening physical ease and stability. It allows you to explore deeper states of consciousness without being pulled back by physical discomfort. Stretching before meditation helps release tension, making it easier to maintain focus during prolonged meditation sessions. It's like tuning an instrument before a performance —you ensure everything is in harmony, ready for the music of meditation to unfold.

There are many yoga traditions including Ashtanga, Iyengar, Hatha, and Vinyasa. My path is rooted in Kundalini Yoga. I have included a few beginner's sets in the appendix as a foundation for your sadhana.

However, I encourage you to explore local yoga classes and discover which practice speaks to your needs and nature.

Another of my favorite yoga sets for sadhana is *Surya Namaskar*, Sun Salutations from the Hatha Yoga tradition. For me, it's the perfect blend of stretch and strength to awaken the body and prevent my legs from falling asleep during meditation.

Use these few yoga sets as a starting point and then expand and integrate the practices that serve you best. If you want to explore Kundalini Yoga further, consider finding a class near you or checking out the e-learning offerings at 3HO or the Kundalini Research Institute.[iv]

LAYA YOGA - THE POWER OF CHANTING MANTRA

Laya Yoga, the meditation of chanting mantra, is a discipline in which sound dissolves individual consciousness into the Universal, quieting the mind and opening it to internal wisdom.

The mind's habitual movement gradually settles through the repetition of mantra, leading to a state of internal stillness beyond ordinary thought. When sustained with concentration, the vibration of sound harmonizes the subtle energies of the body and mind, facilitating the withdrawal of awareness from the external to the internal.

In traditional Laya Yoga, mantra is not viewed as mere repetition of words, but as a vibrational method to transcend the egoic mind. Each sound is designed to resonate within the practitioner, dissolving mental constructs and reorienting consciousness toward its original, undifferentiated state. Over time, the practitioner experiences a progressive merging of the personal self into the formless Absolute. The consistent practice of Laya Yoga refines mental clarity and strengthens the capacity for sustained meditative absorption.

There are thousands of mantras, and the one you use in your sadhana can be based on your religious tradition. Mantra meditation invites us to explore our inner landscapes, guiding us toward clarity and tranquility.

There are four mantras inspired by the Sikh tradition included in the appendix for you to try. Some of these are in the form of a *kriya*, based on the teachings of Yogi Bhajan, combining breath, posture, and mudra to enhance the effectiveness of the mantra. They are:

- Mul Mantra
- Ek Ong Kaar, Sat Nam, Siri Waheguru
- Sohung
- Sa-Ta-Na-Ma

Whichever mantra you choose—whether chanted aloud or silently with the breath—commit to it consistently for the time you choose. Trust your intuition to guide you when it's time to adjust the duration or the mantra itself.

END YOUR SADHANA WITH A PRAYER OF GRATITUDE

As you conclude your sadhana, take a moment to reflect and appreciate. Gratitude acts like a balm for the soul, soothing and enriching every facet of your being. It's more than just saying thank you; it's acknowledging the journey inward, honoring the progress and peace you've cultivated. This is where your practice comes full circle, an opportunity to recognize the subtle shifts within that ripple outward into your daily life.

This practice of gratitude enriches your sadhana. It invites you to see beyond the immediate benefits, fostering a deeper understanding of your interconnectedness with everything. Incorporating gratitude into your sadhana cultivates a mindset that carries into everyday life. Finding things you're thankful for becomes second nature, even in the most mundane moments. This shift in perspective enhances relationships, boosts overall well-being, and builds strength in the face of life's challenges. Gratitude acts as a lens through which you view the world, highlighting abundance rather than lack, joy rather than sorrow. It's a simple practice that enriches each day, turning routine experiences into opportunities for connection and joy.

As we conclude this chapter, remember that sadhana is about more than meditation; it's about creating a life imbued with intention and focus. Each step in your practice, from invocation to gratitude,is a building block for a more aware and connected existence. Let gratitude be your guide, illuminating your steps with warmth and wisdom as you continue this path of self-discovery and growth.

———

5
DEEP RELAXATION - YOGA NIDRA

Picture this: you have had one of those days where your mind feels like a tangled ball of yarn, knotted and frayed. You long for a moment of respite to unravel and find peace. This is a perfect time for *Yoga Nidra*. It's a practice that whispers, "Rest here, let go." Lie down and let the gentle guidance of a voice lead you into a state of profound relaxation. It's as if your body is asleep, but your mind stays awake, floating in a serene sea. Yoga Nidra is a great way to end your sadhana when you have time.

EMBRACING THE ART OF CONSCIOUS REST

While daily commitments may not always allow for a full Yoga Nidra session with sadhana, even brief encounters with this practice can offer powerful benefits. You don't have to wait for the perfect moment or setting. Sometimes, a quick session during lunch or before bed can work wonders. It's about finding those pockets of time where you can dive into this oasis of stillness and emerge refreshed.

Yoga Nidra adapts to your needs with flexible scripts that cater to different settings and time constraints, making it an ideal companion for anyone seeking tranquility. Whether you have 15 minutes or an hour, there's a version of Yoga Nidra that fits perfectly into your day. Short scripts are great for quick stress relief when time is tight, offering a concentrated dose of calm. When your schedule allows, longer sessions deepen relaxation, guiding you into a restorative state that rejuvenates both body and spirit.

As you lie there, the world outside fades, and you embark on an inner journey. You start by setting an intention, a *sankalpa*, that serves as a guiding light through the practice. This intention aligns with your heart, planting seeds for transformation and healing. Then, your awareness is guided systematically through different body parts, releasing tension and inviting relaxation.

Your breath becomes the anchor, grounding you in the present moment. As the breath flows effortlessly, you detach from the emotional and sensory clutter that often dominates waking life. In this space between wakefulness and sleep, visualization opens doors to the subconscious, allowing symbolic imagery to surface and guide your experience.

The beauty of Yoga Nidra lies in its simplicity and profound impact on stress relief and emotional regulation. It invites rest by activating the parasympathetic nervous system. A mere 30 minutes can mimic hours of sleep in terms of restoration, leaving you feeling renewed and balanced.

Beyond immediate relaxation, Yoga Nidra offers emotional healing by providing a safe space to observe and process feelings without becoming overwhelmed or identified with them. This process supports nervous system balance and enhances immune function by promoting homeostasis. In this state, the body's systems operate optimally.

In Y0ga Nidra, you access brainwave frequencies associated with deep rest and healing, theta and delta waves, where subconscious material emerges for integration and transformation. Your sankalpa becomes an ally in this process, nurturing personal growth by planting intentions in the fertile soil of your subconscious mind.

On weekends, when you have extra time in the morning, Yoga Nidra is a great practice to do after completing your sadhana. For those who struggle with sleep or insomnia, Yoga Nidra before bed trains the body to relax deeply. It unwinds mental overactivity and eases anxiety, creating a bridge to restful sleep that eludes many.

What is Yoga Nidra?

Yoga Nidra, often referred to as "yogic sleep" or "deep relaxation," is a practice that combines a unique blend of relaxation and awareness. It's like a reset button for the mind and body. Your body lies comfortably in *Shavasana*, "corpse pose," where you are lying flat with your arms at your sides. At the same time, a gentle voice guides you through layers of relaxation. Unlike traditional meditation, where you might sit and focus on your breathing or a mantra, Yoga Nidra lets you lie down. The body rests as the mind stays awake, floating between wakefulness and sleep.

This practice originates from ancient yogic traditions, with roots dating back to sacred texts depicting deities like Lord Vishnu in a state of Yoga Nidra, symbolizing balance and preservation. It's often said that even as the universe rests, it remains conscious—a cosmic metaphor for this meditative practice. As you engage with Yoga Nidra, consider it a passageway into a restful state, where the usual boundaries of conscious thought gently dissolve.

The essence of Yoga Nidra lies in its ability to guide you through various stages of relaxation without losing awareness. As you progress, the practice involves a systematic body scan, where attention moves across each body part. Breath awareness plays a pivotal role, anchoring you in the present moment. As you breathe deeply, thoughts settle, allowing emotional and sensory detachment to unfold naturally. It's a space where you observe without reacting, a witness to your experience.

Visualization takes this journey further by engaging the subconscious through symbolic imagery. Here, the mind's eye becomes a canvas, painting pictures that resonate with more profound truths. You might be guided to imagine walking through a serene forest or floating on a tranquil sea. These images speak to parts of you that are often hidden beneath your daily consciousness, offering insights and healing.

HOW TO ADD YOGA NIDRA TO YOUR PRACTICE

Yoga Nidra is a guided meditation, with a voice that takes you to each stage of relaxation, step by step. All you need is a place to lie flat, the floor, a couch, or your bed, and a way to stream a Yoga Nidra session online. Fortunately, there are many beautiful, guided meditations available on YouTube. Here are three to start your exploration of this relaxation practice, but feel free to look online and find the one just right for you:

15 Minute Yoga Nidra | Guided Meditation for Beginners

Led by Cyrena Guyot from Pacific Prana Yoga, this beginner-friendly practice guides you through a relaxing body scan and breath awareness, making it accessible for those new to Yoga Nidra. Watch it here:

20 Minute Yoga Nidra: Guided Meditation to Relax and Restore

This guided meditation, led by Caren Hope, offers a comprehensive journey through the stages of Yoga Nidra. It's suitable for newcomers and seasoned practitioners aiming to deepen their practice. Watch it here:

30 Minute Yoga Nidra: Guided Meditation to Relax & Rejuvenate

This entire session, led by Anandmurti Gurumaa, explores the traditional roots of Yoga Nidra, emphasizing relaxation, rejuvenation, and mental clarity. It includes visualizations and is perfect for those interested in the practice's deeply spiritual dimensions. Watch it here:

6

THE SADHANA MINDSET
STRATEGIES FOR MAINTAINING CONSISTENCY

L ife can throw curveballs that disrupt even the best-laid plans. You've probably experienced this—an unexpected work deadline demands immediate attention, or family obligations suddenly shift and pull you away from your routine. Illness can sap your energy, making the thought of meditating seem impossible. And travel can upend your schedule, leaving you without your usual space or support. These challenges can make consistency seem elusive, but they're not insurmountable.

Establish regular meditation times despite occasional disruptions. Think of these as appointments with yourself. It becomes an anchor in your day, providing stability amidst chaos. Also, consider enlisting a meditation partner for accountability. Having someone else involved can increase your commitment and knowing that a partner is counting on you can be a powerful motivator. This shared commitment can turn meditation from a solitary pursuit into a shared experience, providing support and encouragement when needed.

Your mindset plays an essential role in maintaining consistency. Emphasize the benefits of regular meditation to yourself, how it improves focus, reduces stress, and enhances well-being. This awareness strengthens your resolve, even when distractions abound.

Select a time when interruptions are least likely, such as early morning or late evening. Create an environment that signals tranquility; a consistent and graceful sadhana space. Setting boundaries with family or room-mates is essential, too. Let them know your meditation time is sacred, an appointment with yourself that should not be disturbed. This may require gentle reminders, but it reinforces the importance of your practice.

Effective time management is about prioritizing what matters most. View meditation not as an optional add-on but as a key activity in your day. It's like brushing your teeth—something you do to maintain health and well-being. Block out specific times for meditation in your schedule, treating them as non-negotiable appointments. This commitment makes it easier to prioritize amidst a sea of tasks and responsibilities.

And when you miss sadhana, practice self-compassion. Missing a session doesn't mean failure; it's simply an opportunity to learn and adjust. Treat yourself with kindness and understanding, recognizing that unpredictability is a regular part of life. Quick recovery strategies can help you get back on track when disruptions occur. Short catch-up meditations can be invaluable; even five minutes can restore your sense of balance. Reflecting on a missed sadhana allows you to identify patterns and understand what caused you to deviate from your course. This reflection isn't about self-criticism, but rather about gaining insight into managing your time and commitments more effectively in the future.

In my journey with sadhana, I have experienced extended gaps without daily meditation. Things that come to mind are periods of ill health, work deadlines, and a time of grief and depression. Even knowing that meditation would make me feel better, I couldn't bring myself to sit with myself. But during these trying periods, my *intention* was always to return to my sadhana. I missed it, and I thought of it with longing. In my heart, I never left it. So, when grace returned to life, I eagerly sat before my altar again.

When you face personal difficulties, don't give up. Remember, perfection isn't the goal; persistence is. Each day offers a fresh start, an opportunity to recommit to your sadhana with renewed dedication and understanding. Incorporating these strategies can make consistency more achievable. It provides a framework to navigate life's ups and downs without losing sight of what truly matters. By embracing a sadhana mindset, you cultivate a practice that endures, offering a steady source of peace and clarity amidst the storm.

ADAPTING YOUR PRACTICE TO LIFE'S CHANGES

Life has a funny way of keeping us on our toes. Just when you think you've settled into a routine, everything shifts. Whether stepping into the world of parenthood or adjusting to a new work schedule, these changes require flexibility. Meditation, while a steady anchor, benefits from adaptability. Each life phase offers unique challenges and opportunities. Parenthood, for instance, might mean shorter meditations but ones steeped in gratitude, all found in the quiet moments before the household wakes. A new work environment could invite fresh perspectives and even new meditation spots that inspire reflection. Embracing these transitions rather than resisting them can enrich your practice.

When life changes, modify your meditation practice. Adjusting goals and expectations allows you to maintain momentum without feeling overwhelmed. You could switch from a longer sadhana to a series of shorter ones scattered throughout the day. Adaptations ensure that meditation continues to serve you, offering peace and clarity amid life's unpredictability.

Resilience is your ally and your superpower. Meditation cultivates mental fortitude, equipping you with the tools to navigate change more easily. It teaches you to remain centered, even when the external world is in flux. Embracing change as part of spiritual growth enables you to view transitions as opportunities for deeper understanding, rather than obstacles. Each challenge faced and overcome strengthens your resolve, deepening your commitment to the path you've chosen.

By adapting your meditation practice to life's changes, you are not just adjusting routines; you are nurturing growth.

Don't Give Up!

Persisting through challenges pays off in ways you might not expect. The initial fatigue gives way to a newfound energy and clarity that permeates your day. As your body adapts to this routine, you'll discover a deeper connection to yourself, a quiet strength that carries you through. Remember, sadhana is about nurturing your spirit, not punishing it.

Celebrate each small victory along the way and trust that these early mornings hold gifts that are only revealed with time. As your sadhana becomes a steady rhythm in your life, you'll notice that something begins to shift. The relentless dialogue of the mind softens, giving way to moments of silence and gratitude. In that silence, a deeper awareness stirs, one that is not caught in roles and stories but rooted in the unchanging Self. From this space of consciousness, the heart begins to open, not as a concept but as a lived experience. In the chapters ahead, we will explore how sadhana quiets the mind's noise, reveals the luminous core of your being, and awakens the heart to the fullness of life. These are not abstract ideals, they are the natural gifts of showing up, day after day, in devotion to your own spiritual growth.

> *When you do sadhana, you control your mind and purify yourself. There is no corruption, there is no dirt, there is no rust, there are no cobwebs. Yogi Bhajan 7/13/1983*

————

7
QUIETING THE NOISE OF THE MIND
SADHANA'S SILENT REWARD

When you begin your sadhana practice, expect the mind to wander. This is a natural part of meditation, not a sign of failure on your part, and it happens to all of us. Instead of responding with frustration, notice the thoughts, name them ("That is a thought!"), and gently bring your focus back to your breath or mantra.

At times, deeper emotions may surface, such as anger, frustration, or old wounds that are difficult to ignore. This, too, is part of the process. In meditation, old and often unresolved thoughts rise to the forefront as a way of being cleared from the psyche. Yogi Bhajan used to call it "taking out the garbage." The key is neither to suppress nor to indulge these thoughts; see them, name them, and allow them to pass without attachment. This clearing does not occur immediately but rather unfolds over time. As the mind gradually releases these old patterns, genuine healing takes place. And when these burdens are released, they do not return. Of course, the mind contains many layers, and the purification process will last a lifetime. But just as physical fitness rewards consistent effort, mental clarity and emotional freedom are well worth the dedication that sadhana requires.

Rest assured that at the heart of meditation there lies a sacred stillness where thought fades, the self dissolves, and one merges with the silent rhythm of the Universe. This is called *shunya*.

SHUNYA: THE STILLNESS WITHIN ALL THINGS

Shunya, often called *emptiness* or *void*, does not signify absence, but rather a dynamic space of silent potential—the fertile ground from which creation arises. This begins to hint at the meaning of shunya, an ancient concept embedded in traditions such as Vedanta, Buddhism, Yoga, and Sikhism.

In Advaita Vedanta, shunya is closely aligned with *Brahman*, the unchanging, formless reality underlying all phenomena. It is not the void of nothingness but of stillness, a substrate of existence beneath the changing forms of life.

In Madhyamika Buddhism, shunya denotes the emptiness inherent in existence. It teaches that no object or being possesses an independent essence; all things arise *inter*dependently. Realizing this leads not to nihilism, but to liberation, a freedom from clinging to the dual illusions of separation and permanence.

Yoga approaches shunya as the inner space where identity dissolves, leaving pure consciousness to remain. Through deep meditation, practitioners transcend thoughts and ego, entering a realm of silence, clarity, and unity. In this state, the fluctuations of the mind subside, allowing the underlying reality to emerge with quiet certainty.

In Sikhism, *sunn* is intertwined with the teachings of Guru Nanak and Guru Angad. It is described as the primordial statefrom which creation unfolds. Sikh philosophy portrays shunya as a divine fullness; a sacred silence teeming with creative force.

Across these traditions, shunya points not to emptiness but to a profound foundation of being, a silent potential that gives rise to all life and existence. The sadhana experience is an invitation to shunya, a state beyond thought and form, where authentic reality reveals itself.

Why We Seek Inner Stillness

In the noise of daily life, the mind is easily overwhelmed, constantly processing, evaluating, and reacting. This compulsive activity clouds inner clarity and disconnects us from our deeper selves. Stillness is not an escape from life but a return to an essential, enduring state within.

In stillness, we remember that our worth is not tied to external achievements or identities. We peel away the distractions of narrative and performance, reconnecting to a beingness that *is*. Here, we encounter ourselves with compassion, free from the distortions of judgment and comparison.

Shunya offers a radical alternative to modern life, a return to undistracted awareness. In this space, identity loosens its grip, and what remains is pure being—free, expansive, and interconnected. In silence, we are no longer defined by our roles or accomplishments. We rediscover the still point beyond the motion, coherence behind life's surface turbulence. It is not an escape from reality, but a fuller participation in it, unburdened by constant mental struggle.

HOW TO QUIET THE MIND

From a neurological perspective, the mind's restlessness is linked to what scientists call the Default Mode Network (DMN)—a set of brain regions that activate when we are not focused on the external world. The DMN is associated with mind wandering, self-referential thinking, rumination, and narrative construction. This network generates the familiar mental chatter: reviewing the past, imagining the future, rehearsing conversations, or replaying worries.

Meditation does not aim to suppress the DMN by force, but rather to retrain our relationship with it. Research using functional-MRI (fMRI) has demonstrated that regular meditation decreases activity in the brain's DMN. This reduction is correlated with improved emotional regulation and increased present-moment awareness (Garrison et al., 2015).

Through sustained practice, we can gradually quiet the mind's habitual patterns, strengthening networks in the brain associated with focused attention. Spiritual traditions have long understood this challenge intuitively. They offer practices that mirror what neuroscience now confirms that sustained, gentle redirection of attention is the key to transforming mental activity. Helpful methods include:

Focused attention: An effective approach is anchoring awareness on a single object, like the breath, a mantra, or a point of sensation. Each time attention drifts, which it naturally will, we gently and patiently bring it back, strengthening the brain's capacity for focus and regulation.

Visualization: Evoking expansive images, such as an endless sky or still waters, invites the mind into spaciousness, helping to interrupt cycles of contraction and overthinking.

Detached observation: Watching thoughts arise and pass without judgment or attachment fosters emotional regulation and increases our capacity for inner stillness.

One technique that you can use anywhere, anytime is *shunya visualization*:

> *Close your eyes, visualize a vast, infinite sky. Inhale gently and exhale into the limitless expanse. With each exhale, the mind releases a layer of distraction, allowing the still, silent space to emerge gradually.*

Another potent method is *shunya shravana* - "deep listening."

> *Focus within and deeply listen to your surroundings. Hear and name each noise that comes to you from your environment. Extend your awareness to 1,000 meters, and strain to hear the noise of traffic or movement from that distance. Focus intently and extend your "listening" even further – throughout the city, across the entire country, and around the globe. Listen deeper and deeper. Listen so deeply that even the subtlest internal sounds dissolve into stillness. Hear beyond all sounds, into the infinite, resonant stillness of shunya, and remain there.*

In meditation, the goal is not to force silence, but to return to the present moment again and again. In this way, we train the mind not through struggle, but through steady remembrance of the experience of profound stillness. You will find that moments of shunya, of resting in the formlessness beneath thought, begin to arise naturally.

———

8

MASTERING THE MIND
CULTIVATING SELF-AWARENESS
THROUGH SADHANA

"Conquer your mind, and you conquer the world." — *Japji Sahib,*
Pauri 28

This line beautifully encapsulates Guru Nanak's core message that inner mastery is the key to liberation and fulfillment. Inner mastery is the fruit of self-awareness.

Self-awareness is the journey of turning inward, descending beneath the mind's noise to uncover your steady, luminous being beyond roles, achievements, or identities. Through meditation, one gradually awakens to the silent witness within, the aspect of consciousness that observes without judgment and remains unaffected by external circumstances. In this stillness, true sovereignty of the Self is realized, and self-mastery is developed.

Let me clarify that self-mastery, like many aspects of the spiritual path, is a journey, not a destination. We are humans, after all, and resistance, fear, anger, and doubt are part of the human experience and will always be our traveling companions. However, through our sadhana's hard work, we can learn to grasp the concept of personal freedom that comes from recognizing the true Self as separate from these emotions.

In the theater of life, you are not merely the actor but also the observer seated in the audience, calmly witnessing the play unfold. Thoughts and emotions come and go like actors on a stage, but the true Self remains unmoved—eternal, aware, and free. Recognizing the Self is not about cataloging surface-level traits such as preferences, habits, or labels. It is about discovering pure consciousness, the underlying substrate of all mental and emotional activity.

SELF-AWARENESS AS A PILLAR OF SPIRITUAL WISDOM

Across spiritual traditions, self-mastery is not seen as dominance over the Self, but as the realization and integration of one's highest nature through disciplined inner alignment. It is the fruit of a consistent sadhana; the capacity to live as the authentic Self with conscious intent.

In Vedantic wisdom, *atma bodha* ("knowledge of the Self") involves recognizing the atma, the eternal Self, and mastering identification with it, thereby transcending the illusions of ego and mind.

In Sikh thought, *haumai,* or ego-identification, is one of the primary obstacles to spiritual realization. What many call "self" is often just the voice of ego, separateness, and pride. The path of Gurbani points instead toward *atma giaan,* soul-knowledge, fundamental awareness of one's identity as Divine Light, not as a separate, ego-based individual.

In Buddhism, practices such as *Sati* (mindful presence) and *Rigpa* (Dzogchen's non-dual awareness) invite not just recognition, but also stabilization in clarity and freedom from conditioned reactivity, hallmarks of true self-mastery.

In Christian mysticism, the path to *Christ Consciousness* involves surrendering the self, an active transformation through love, humility, and inner purification. Gnostic teachings highlight self-awareness as the experiential realization of the divine Self within.

Despite their diverse expressions, these traditions affirm that self-awareness is not about ego or control, but about conscious alignment with the Eternal—a disciplined return to the true Self that transcends impermanence, where action arises from clarity rather than compulsion.

Developing Reflective Awareness

Reflective awareness is the foundation upon which self-mastery is built. It is the capacity to observe one's thoughts, emotions, and behaviors without immediate reaction, creating space between the stimulus and the response. Through reflective awareness, we recognize the patterns that govern our actions, some inherited and some conditioned. This recognition is the first step toward transformation. Awareness blooms when we consciously direct our inner life and inner dialogue, rather than being driven by unconscious impulses or external expectations. In essence, self-awareness reveals the landscape of the Self, while self-mastery is its skillful navigation. Together, they form the path to spiritual growth and authentic being.

Meditation serves as a mirror to the Self, offering a profound method for self-reflection. By turning inward, we begin to observe the patterns of thought and emotion that subtly shape our behavior. While our mind is focused on breath and mantra, a spontaneous cleansing of the subconscious occurs, peeling back the layers of the conditioned mind, revealing truths hidden beneath habitual responses. This often manifests as unwanted thoughts or emotions that bubble up while we meditate. Over time, you become aware of the root causes of your reactions and emotional fluctuations. What a gift! Once you can identify what is causing you discomfort, you are empowered to make a change.

Sakshi Bhava, or cultivating the "witness consciousness," is a powerful method for deepening this process. Sitting quietly and observing thoughts as passing phenomena without judgment fosters detachment and nurtures an inner spaciousness, allowing self-awareness to expand naturally. Observing thoughts and emotions as a bystander, rather than in the first person, brings great agency to assess the situation truthfully and impact the outcome.

It sounds like a lot of work, but it is easier than you think. When you meditate and give your mind the space it needs for transformation, it often occurs naturally. Your job, and your challenge, is to keep meditating.

FROM REACTION TO CONSCIOUS RESPONSE

Many of us have experienced moments where our reactions seem disproportionate to the situation; snapping at a loved one, withdrawing in silence, or feeling an overwhelming urge to escape a situation. These intense reactions often stem not from the present moment but from unhealed emotional wounds of the past. In the language of modern psychology, these are called *triggers*. A trigger is any stimulus—an image, word, tone, or situation—that unconsciously activates past emotional pain.

Often, these wounds originate in childhood, when our sense of Self was still forming, and our nervous system was highly impressionable. Experiences of neglect, criticism, abandonment, or trauma leave emotional imprints. When something in the present moment mirrors those early pains, the body instinctively responds. The *amygdala*, a part of the brain responsible for processing fear, activates the "fight, flight, or freeze" response. Logic recedes. Emotions surge. The mind perceives itself as under threat, even when it is not.

When we react unconsciously, we often escalate the situation we are trying to avoid. A raised voice is met with defensiveness. A critical remark is met with shame or anger. Our reactions frequently reinforce cycles of suffering in ourselves and others. These emotional loops can entrench relationships in patterns of hurt and mistrust.

So, how do we move from a blind reaction to a conscious response?

An important step is self-awareness. Through daily reflection and sadhana practice, we begin to witness the workings of our mind. Meditation offers a mirror, reflecting the habitual thoughts, emotions, and sensations that drive our behavior. When we have the courage to explore this territory, we learn to recognize our triggers as they arise.

This shift is supported by neuroscience. Mindfulness meditation in the Buddhist tradition, now widely studied, has been shown to reduce activity in the amygdala and strengthen the *prefrontal cortex*—the part of the brain associated with rational decision-making and emotional regulation. In a study published in Psychiatry Research: Neuroimaging, participants who completed an 8-week mindfulness program exhibited measurable changes in their brains, with reduced activity in the region associated with stress and increased activity in areas related to self-awareness. This science supports what ancient traditions have long taught: Awareness changes the brain and our behavior.

Naming our emotional state is one of the most effective tools for transforming our reactions. When we label what we're feeling—"I'm feeling rejected," "This reminds me of not being heard as a child," or "I'm triggered right now," for example—we begin to disidentify from the emotion. It is no longer *me*, but *something moving through me*. This is Sakshi Bhava, or witness consciousness, in action.

Once we become aware, we have a choice. We can pause. This pause is the space between stimulus and response, famously described by Holocaust survivor and psychiatrist Viktor Frankl:

> *"Between stimulus and response, there is a space. In that space, we have the power to choose our response. In our response lies our growth and our freedom."*

This space is not always easy to find, especially in moments of emotional intensity. However, through regular sadhana, we train the nervous system to focus and more easily tolerate discomfort, giving us the power to respond with wisdom rather than reflex.

That is not to say that spiritual practice alone is enough to heal all wounds. Some traumas require professional psychological support. Therapy can help uncover and integrate unconscious material in ways that meditation may not reach. Sadhana and therapy are not opposing paths—they work in harmony. Spiritual practice offers daily discipline, centering, and connection to the Divine, while treatment provides the tools and support to process and heal the emotional body.

The journey from reaction to realization is not about becoming perfectly calm and unemotional. Certainly, not. It involves being present and honest with our emotions. We learn to meet our emotional pain not with fear or avoidance, but with curiosity and compassion. We begin to see that our triggers can be our teachers. They show us where healing is needed, where compassion is lacking, and where inner work can still unfold. As we walk this path, the situations that once caused upheaval become opportunities for insight. We become more patient and forgiving, both of ourselves and others.

Ultimately, self-awareness is not only about recognizing our emotions, but also about adjusting our responses to them. Reaction is the mind in chains; realization is the mind set free. Through daily discipline, spiritual inquiry, and honest reflection, we transform. We learn to respond, not from our wounds, but from our wisdom.

THE IMPACT OF LIVING IN AWARENESS OF THE SELF

To live in awareness of the Self is to walk through life with greater clarity, balance, and inner sovereignty. It is not a state of perfection, nor immunity from challenge, but a cultivated worldview that remains grounded through the shifting tides of experience. This mastery arises not by force, but through the steady discipline of self-examination. With time, this reflective discipline dissolves the hold of the ego and the emotional fluctuations that once dictated our reactions. We gain the capacity to witness life without distortion—to see things not as we wish them to be, or fear them to be, but as they truly are. This clarity of perception becomes the ground for conviction of action: an intuitive knowing that arises without overthinking. We begin to act from intuition, not compulsion.

Inner awareness also frees us from the tyranny of external circumstances. Though challenges will still come, we are no longer victims of time, mood, or fate. Suffering will still arise, but it does not uproot our center. We become anchored in an inner equilibrium that bends with life but remains unbroken.

Importantly, the journey of self-knowledge is not fixed or final. It is a living process. To live in understanding of oneself is to remain attuned to this unfolding, adjusting your compass as needed to stay true to the deeper current of your soul.

Within this rhythm of conscious living, another gift reveals itself: gratitude. Not the kind tied to success or comfort, but a quiet reverence for the hidden blessings woven into the ordinary. Gratitude becomes the fragrance of self-realization; the gentle appreciation of life's sacred unfolding in every breath, every pause, every step. Gratitude has been linked to improved psychological well-being, further supporting the transformative journey.

Self-awareness is not a finish line. It is a lifelong devotion to living with intentionality, compassion, and sacred presence. It is the flowering of sadhana, not just in meditation but also in how we think, speak, and walk through the world. This journey requires patience, gentleness, and inner strength. However, with each moment of awareness, our connection to life deepens, our lives become fuller, our relationships more authentic, and our actions more aligned with truth.

Seeking self-realization is not about becoming someone new. It is about becoming more fully who you are, beyond roles, stories, and conditions. We do not lose ourselves; we meet ourselves, perhaps for the first time. That meeting is a special kind of freedom, a quiet liberation that grows from a daily sadhana.

————

9

AN OPEN HEART
AWAKENING DEVOTION AND INTUITION

An open heart is not an anomaly—it is our natural state. We are designed to live with hearts wide open, to feel deeply, and to love freely. Just look at a mother's instinctive love for her child, or how a lover gazes upon their beloved with devotion. This capacity to love unconditionally is not learned; it is intrinsically woven into the fabric of our being. However, as we move through life disappointment and fear begin to build walls around that original openness. We learn to protect ourselves, to guard the heart, and in doing so, we forget the ease and beauty of living with vulnerability and grace.

What if we could return to that natural state? What if the walls could soften, and the heart could breathe again? A daily spiritual practice can help you gradually return to your true nature. Through devotion, meditation, and inner discipline, sadhana becomes a path back to the openhearted living we were created for.

A consistent sadhana affects the practitioner's body and mind in many ways, but none so profound as the opening of the heart center. Although some physiology is involved, this is primarily an energetic opening, releasing the illusion of separation and allowing life in its fullness to move through us and transform us. A regular meditation practice supports this process, clearing the mind's unnecessary defensive reactions, reducing anxiety in the body, and allowing the full range of life's input to be received by the human consciousness.

Sadhana awakens us to the facility of insight and intuition. When we see life more as it is and less through our lens of fear and insecurity, an unexpected thing happens – devotion arises. I say surprising, because in this age of logic and reason, conscious devotion is not something we are often exposed to. Nevertheless, there it is, love in an abstract form that fills your being and changes everything you thought you knew.

The yogic tradition has a very in-depth psychospiritual physiology system that includes the heart center, known as the *chakras*. Chakras are subtle energy centers within the body corresponding to specific physical, emotional, and spiritual functions, aligned along the spine. The fourth chakra is known as the Heart Chakra, also called *Anahata*. Writings on chakras are a vast body of information and are not included here. However, I encourage you to delve deeper into that topic through the many excellent books that are available.

DEVOTION ACROSS TRADITIONS

Across the world's religions, we see the devotional current of the heart center expressed in diverse yet strikingly resonant ways. In Hinduism, *bhakti yoga* offers a path to spiritual union through heartfelt love for the Divine, expressed through song, prayer, and surrender. In Christianity, the image of Christ's Sacred Heart symbolizes a profound, divine love that encompasses suffering for the sake of others. In Islam, the Sufi mystics whirl in remembrance of the Beloved, their hearts inflamed with longing. Buddhism offers devotion to the Buddha, bodhisattvas, and the ideal of awakened compassion.

In Sikhism, devotion is a central path to merging with the Divine through *Naam Simran*—the remembrance of God's Name, vibrating through an open heart. Guru Nanak Dev ji, the founder of the Sikh faith, emerged in the Punjab region during the 15th century, a time of profound religious, cultural, and political upheaval. His spiritual message was rooted in a direct experience of the Divine and expressed in a deeply devotional form that resonates with the Bhakti tradition—a pan-Indic spiritual movement emphasizing love, devotion, and a personal relationship with God.

What unites these paths is not theology, but the posture of the heart. Whether bowing before a form, a formless mystery, or a set of sacred principles, the essence of devotion is the same: to soften the heart, surrender to ego, and become permeable to something greater than yourself.

INTUITION AND INNER INSIGHT

Modern science tends to see the heart as a mechanical pump. However, in spiritual traditions, and increasingly in scientific fields such as neuro-cardiology, the heart is understood as much more; a seat of awareness, intuition, and interconnection.

Research by the HeartMath Institute has demonstrated that the heart possesses its own intrinsic nervous system and communicates with the brain to influence emotional processing, decision-making, and perception. States of "heart coherence," cultivated through breath and focus, have been linked to improved emotional regulation and intuitive insight (McCraty et al., 2009).

When the heart center is open and attuned, it becomes an organ of spiritual perception, a doorway to direct knowing that bypasses linear thought. This is why intuitive insights often come not from the head but from the heart.

As we progress on the path of sadhana, we become increasingly sensitive to life's subtle movements. We gain refined perception, and decisions are influenced more by inner alignment than mental calculation. As we begin to trust that sense of truth, inner knowing takes a larger role in our lives. This is intuition—the whisper of consciousness moving through a clear heart. Intuition is not fantasy or sentimentality. It arises from a grounded, embodied awareness cultivated through stillness and trust. It helps us discern what is real, what is needed, and what is life-affirming, not just for ourselves, but for the whole.

Intuition is not a crystal ball that reveals the future but a deepened perception of the rich, layered, and multi-dimensional present. Intuition lets us sense life's subtle undercurrents and perceive information beyond the five senses. It is not mystical in the fantastical sense, but a natural extension of the human mind's potential. Sometimes it may feel like foresight or prescience, but it is actually a heightened view of what is already unfolding. I think it is everyday magic—an inner knowing that guides us with clarity and quiet wisdom.

Not long ago, I was walking a mountain path in Japan, a sacred pilgrimage route in the Taoist tradition. The landscape was quiet and reverent, with ancient shrines wrapped in mist. As I walked, my heart felt open and fully tuned to the spirit of the place. I paused to rest in a grove of tall cypress trees with their grounding and ethereal presence. As a remembrance, I scooped up a small handful of tiny cypress cones from the forest floor. To my great surprise, a small gold and diamond earring was nestled among the cones.

Gold and diamonds were found unexpectedly amidst cypress cones.

It felt like a gift from the mountain, a recognition of my presence and state of mind. Although I was unaware of the gold's gleam in the leaves, some deeper part of me must have seen it. This knowing is intuition: a quiet, unseen thread of connection that opens when we are receptive, when the heart is whole and the mind still. I keep that earring and cypress cones on my altar, a reminder of the subtle blessings that come when you least expect them.

TUNING INTO CONSCIOUSNESS IN ITS PRIMARY FORM

As the heart center opens, we touch consciousness in its primary form, not as thought or self-reflection but as pure beingness. Before mind, emotion, and belief, there is awareness. It is spacious, loving, and nonjudgmental. And it is always here.

A growing philosophical and scientific theory, known as panpsychism, proposes that consciousness is not merely a byproduct of complex brains but a fundamental aspect of reality, as intrinsic to the universe as space, time, or matter. Rather than seeing consciousness as something that emerges only in human or animal brains, panpsychism suggests that it is present beyond existence, that even the smallest particles of matter possess a form of consciousness. This view challenges materialist assumptions and aligns with many mystical and spiritual traditions, which have long held that consciousness permeates all existence. Panpsychism affirms that when we quiet the mind and soften the boundaries of self, we are not accessing something personal or imagined —we are tapping into a universal field of consciousness that exists in and through all things.

The Open Heart as a Way of Life

Opening the heart is not just a moment in meditation, it is a way of being in the world. It means relating to others with kindness, seeing the Divine in all, and walking with humility and gratitude. It is not passive. The open heart is strong, discerning, and willing to act and sacrifice in the pursuit of truth. It responds not from reactivity, but from wisdom and love. To open the heart is to say yes to life, not just the beautiful moments, but also the broken ones. It is to feel deeply and to be moved by the sacredness of existence. Ultimately, the journey of devotion is not toward something far away. It is a remembering of the love that is always within us, of the reality that never left. The heart, as it opens, does not just receive life. It radiates it.

10

MEETING DOUBT AND EMBRACING CHALLENGES

D oubt is a common and often inevitable part of the spiritual path. It tends to arise when you least expect it, questioning the process, the outcome, or the practitioner's capacity. Whether it appears as uncertainty about technique, skepticism about results, or self-comparison with others, doubt often signals a deeper engagement with the inner journey. It is not a sign of failure, but of sincere inquiry. Recognizing doubt as part of the discipline transforms it from a barrier into a catalyst for deepening understanding. Doubt may challenge the principles of meditation itself, or it may take a more subtle form, such as self-doubt, undermining confidence, progress, or one's sense of worthiness. Rather than avoiding doubt or viewing it as a weakness, we can begin to see it as an invitation to clarify our purpose, strengthen our faith, and recommit to our practice. It offers an opportunity to engage more fully with the teachings and one's growth.

Addressing doubt begins with acknowledgment. When resistance arises, observe it without judgment. Allow it to be present while choosing not to identify with its conclusions. Reframing doubt as a natural stage of development opens the door to greater understanding.

Conversations with experienced practitioners can also bring insight and encouragement. Many have walked through similar periods of questioning and emerged with renewed clarity. In these shared reflections, we find perspective and reassurance. Hearing others share their struggles and breakthroughs reinforces that spiritual growth is not a straight path. It moves through cycles; expansion and contraction, clarity and confusion. In this light, doubt becomes a force that asks us to refine our intention and reconnect with our original inspiration.

Stories from spiritual traditions consistently reflect this truth. Even those who attained great spiritual insight often encountered dark periods of doubt along the way. Their perseverance in the face of uncertainty becomes a source of encouragement. Through steady practice and inner reflection, they found clarity not in avoiding doubt, but in working through it. Their lives affirm that sustained effort and sincere questioning can lead to transformation.

Setting realistic expectations is essential in navigating this process. Progress in meditation is often gradual. Small breakthroughs are not insignificant, they are the building blocks of a stable foundation. Although moments of insight or stillness may be brief, they can carry profound significance. By honoring the incremental nature of change, we increase compassion toward ourselves. Each session, regardless of its apparent success, contributes to the refinement of attention and the cultivation of inner stillness.

Comparison with others can distort our perception of progress. Every practitioner moves through their journey at a unique pace, influenced by personal history, temperament, and life circumstances. Observing this diversity fosters humility and patience. Instead of measuring yourself against external benchmarks, focus on your own experience and the sincerity of your effort. This shift supports self-trust and strengthens endurance.

Community support systems also help anchor your sadhana during times of doubt. Books, recordings, and guided meditations offer guidance and can reinvigorate motivation. Participation in group discussions encourages accountability and reflection. These resources remind us that we are not isolated, but part of a larger community engaged in the same inner work.

EMBRACING CHALLENGES AS OPPORTUNITIES FOR GROWTH

Fear, anger, anxiety, and frustration are inherent to the human experience. As Jim Morrison of the rock band The Doors said, *"No one here gets out alive."*

As you encounter adversity on the path of sadhana, you gain insights into your strength and the depth of your spirit. Through these trials, you develop a robust character that flourishes in uncertainty. Embrace challenges, for they are your greatest teachers.

Reframing adversity requires a shift in perspective. What if, instead of seeing a setback as a failure, you viewed it as a stepping-stone? This shift transforms a hurdle into a platform for growth. Practicing gratitude for these learning experiences can show us the path ahead. Each challenge becomes a lesson in perseverance, teaching you to appreciate the journey as much as the destination. Spiritual teachers often remind us that setbacks are a chance to deepen our understanding and compassion for ourselves. These narratives illuminate the transformative power of persistence.

In this dance with challenges, you learn to welcome change with open arms. Each obstacle presents an opportunity to refine your practice and strengthen your resolve. By fostering a growth mindset, you transform sadhana from a routine ritual into a dynamic process of evolution and self-discovery. Embrace each challenge with courage, knowing it is integral to your spiritual path. Through this lens, difficulties become valuable allies.

Sustaining Energy and Focus in Meditation

Many encounter the challenge of maintaining energy and concentration during meditation. Fatigue, restlessness, and distractions are common, especially when the demands of daily life accumulate. Physical tiredness, poor sleep, or excessive stimulation can make it challenging to enter a meditative state while maintaining alertness. Awareness of these influences allows us to respond with care and intelligent adaptation.

Establishing healthy sleep habits is important. Restful sleep replenishes energy and enhances emotional regulation, both essential for sustained meditation. Simple bedtime routines help signal the body to transition into rest, such as reading spiritual literature or practicing gentle breath awareness before sleep. It may be beneficial for you to listen to spiritual music while you sleep. For me, nothing is more soothing than falling asleep to the sound of *Gurbani Kirtan*. And if I awaken briefly at night, I hear this divine music, allowing me to slip easily back into a restful state. Over time, this strengthens your ability to wake up refreshed and begin your morning practice with presence.

Hydration and nutrition also influence clarity. Drinking enough water throughout the day and eating balanced meals help stabilize the nervous system. Avoiding excess sugar and caffeine may reduce fluctuations in energy that can disrupt the stillness required for meditation. A well-supported body lays the groundwork for a steady and attentive mind.

Above all, self-compassion is essential. There will be days of distraction and doubt. This is natural. Rather than interpreting these moments as failure, view them as part of the process. With time and consistent effort, both clarity and concentration deepen. The path doesn't unfolds all at once, but gradually with each conscious step.

The Effects of Drugs and Alcohol on Your Sadhana

Substances like alcohol and certain recreational drugs may initially seem to enhance relaxation or reduce anxiety. However, the long-term impact of regular use tends to contradict the objectives of a meditative practice.

The truth is that recreational drugs and alcohol, while offering temporary relief from pressure or boredom, often erect towering barriers to achieving the core goals of meditation. These substances, though alluring in their promise of pleasure, can distort perception to the extent that they muddy the waters of self-awareness and disrupt the delicate balance of mind and body.

Take alcohol, for instance. Known as a depressant, it works insidiously to dull mental acuity and inhibit emotional responsiveness, not only in the moment but for several days to follow. On a surface level, it might feel like alcohol takes the edge off life's stresses, but it often leaves a lingering residue of dullness and emotional reactiveness in its wake. This pervasive haze can impede your ability to connect deeply with your inner self during meditation, turning what should be a journey of exploration into a formidable struggle against inertia and self-imposed obfuscation.

Similarly, recreational drugs might offer momentary experiences of euphoria or altered states of consciousness that seem appealing. Yet, these fleeting experiences often come at a cost. They can distort your perception of reality, leading you away from genuine insights and the profound spiritual growth that can be achieved through a committed meditative discipline.

One of the negative results from the casual use of drugs or alcohol is that it is challenging to get up in the early morning and be mentally present to meditate. So, if you are serious about maintaining a consistent sadhana, let that be a priority over temporary moments of relief.

If you're earnestly committed to deepening your meditative practice, consider exploring alternative and healthier ways to achieve relaxation. Yoga or tai chi can help release pent-up tension without compromising mental clarity. Incorporate relaxation techniques such as Yoga Nidra, which calms the mind while preserving awareness.

Always remember that the journey toward sobriety and the path of sadhana is uniquely personal for everyone and no single solution fits all. Allow yourself ample room for mistakes and inevitable setbacks while remaining focused on your overarching intention of spiritual growth. Each day offers a precious opportunity to realign with your core values and reconnect with your authentic self through consistent and intentional meditation.

Cultivating Patience and Perseverance

Patience in meditation means understanding the ebb and flow of practice. It's about letting go of the urge to rush or force results and instead trusting the process. With patience, each session becomes an opportunity to explore the present moment, knowing that progress often comes in subtle, incremental waves.

Perseverance pairs naturally with patience, helping you navigate the inevitable obstacles that arise. Remember that perseverance is not about pushing through at all costs but maintaining a steady commitment and intention to continue your practice.

Patience and perseverance are twin pillars supporting your sadhana practice. They provide stability and resilience, enabling you to delve into the depths of meditation with confidence and a sense of curiosity. Every day of sadhana becomes an opportunity to learn and grow, shaping a path that's uniquely yours. With these qualities as your foundation, you can face whatever challenges arise.

SHAKTI PAD – WHEN DOUBT CONFRONTS MASTERY

Shakti Pad is a stage of development between disciplined practice and mastery, where the seeker is tested by ego, doubt, and spiritual identity. There is no escaping this stage; it comes to everyone who journeys on the path of sadhana. As explained by KRI,

[Shakti Pad] is the most crucial, transitional, and challenging of all the stages of spiritual development. The choices made here, and the transformation that occurs, determine whether the practitioner will progress towards mastery, stay at apprentice levels, or quit the study altogether. It is easy to forget ourselves at this stage and become hypnotized by the satisfaction and power of the skills we have gained. If we surrender to the path and the goal we began our study to fulfill, we will emerge with strength, empowered with an unshakable direction.[i]

In Shakti Pad, one may experience increased energy, insight, or influence, yet face temptations to misuse that power or abandon the path altogether. It is a time when spiritual ambition can inflate the sense of self, creating confusion between genuine guidance and personal projection. Shakti Pad is not a spiritual failure but an unavoidable growth stage. Progress through this stage relies on humility, devotion, and continued alignment with the teachings, not just in word but in lived experience. To pass through Shakti Pad is to surrender the illusion of personal control. Only then does one move beyond this threshold into true spiritual maturity.

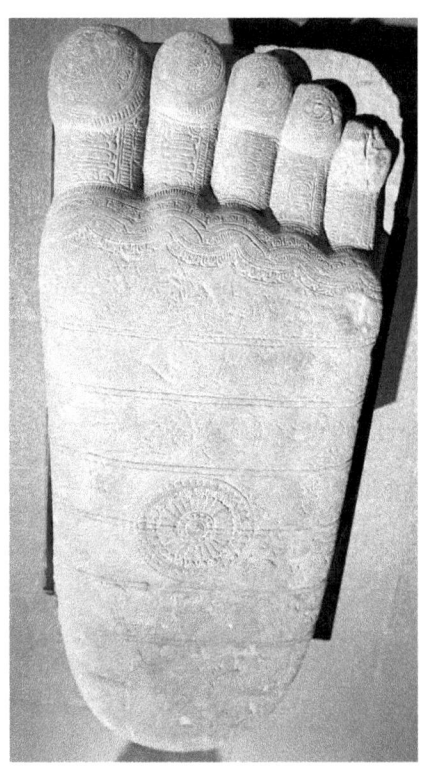

11

THE SPIRITUAL TEACHER
A CHANGING LANDSCAPE OF SPIRITUAL GUIDANCE

From the corridors of history to the hearts of modern seekers, spiritual teachers and guides have upheld the living tradition of sadhana. Their duty extends beyond preserving ancient teachings to adapting and renewing these traditions so their resonance with the evolving world is never lost. This transcendent theater of tradition and modernity is not a deadlock of opposites but a dance, a harmonious existence where each step enriches the fabric of spiritual understanding.

THE TRADITION OF THE SPIRITUAL TEACHER

The *guru-shishya* model is a foundational paradigm in many spiritual and philosophical traditions, including Hinduism, Buddhism, Sufism, and Sikhism. It refers to the sacred relationship between a guru (spiritual teacher or master) and a shishya (disciple or student), through which wisdom, practices, and spiritual realization are transmitted.

The teacher is not just an instructor of knowledge but a living embodiment of the teachings. The student enters the relationship with reverence, devotion, and humility, recognizing that the ego must surrender to undergo true change. Surrender is not blind obedience but a conscious offering of the self to the path of realization, trusting that the teacher points to the deeper truth beyond the mind.

This relationship is seen as sacred and enduring, often lasting a lifetime, or even across lifetimes in some belief systems. The guru-shishya model is not a hierarchical command structure, it is a sacred relationship based on spiritual maturity and mutual respect. The teacher is seen as a mirror, reflecting the true Self of the student and guiding them to that realization through discipline, devotion, and grace.

Navigating the Sea of Information

In Western Europe and the Americas, the traditional model of the spiritual teacher gained widespread interest in the mid-20th century, particularly with the arrival of Eastern traditions. While it still exists today, it has diminished in visibility and influence, with many seekers now favoring self-directed spiritual paths over formal teacher-disciple relationships. This has led to a boundless ocean of information accessible on the internet. It teems with potential but is also fraught with the peril of false and partial information. It is a domain requiring more than passive consumption to traverse confidently. Within it are myriad paths—some routes lead to mere surface engagement, absent of deeper spiritual immersion. Other deeper and more profound paths demand discernment, attention, and guidance to find the treasures of true wisdom nestled within.

While self-guided spiritual practice is possible and sometimes necessary, it carries inherent challenges. Without the guidance of a teacher, there is a greater risk of misinterpreting the teachings or engaging in unskillful practices that deviate from the intended path. A qualified teacher offers clarity and a living transmission of wisdom rooted in experience. Additionally, the absence of external accountability for the student can lead to inconsistency or complacency in practice. One may unknowingly fall prey to subtle forms of ego, spiritual pride, or delusion when practicing alone.

These changes to spiritual learning have created both a challenge and an opportunity. Where knowledge once flowed linearly from teacher to student, it now swirls in currents of shared perspectives and energized dialogues between students. Here is an arena where ideas grow both in minds and between them, allowing collective insights to shape individual understandings. The Buddha exhorted his disciples to have collective dialogues to preserve the purity of the teachings. He said:

> *"Monks, this spiritual life is lived with association as the first requisite. And how does this association come about? By reliance on a good friend, reliance on a good companion, reliance on a good brother." (Samyutta Nikaya 45.2)*

Within this new learning ethos lies uncharted potential for those delving into sadhana. Here, the traditional guru-disciple dynamic reimagines itself, where the distribution of knowledge becomes an inclusive circle of students rather than a hierarchical ladder. Such spaces allow seekers to cross-pollinate ideas, exploring together to unearth wisdom that stands unmoved against the evolving tides.

A Guide on Your Path

Navigating the vast terrain of meditation can feel like embarking on an epic journey through an unimagined landscape. On this journey, a spiritual teacher emerges not just as a guide but as a compass, an experienced explorer, and a companion whose presence is as comforting as it is enlightening. The role they play in guiding, nurturing, and profoundly deepening your practice transcends simple instruction.

To truly embark on a voyage of self-discovery, you must step into the realm of vulnerability, an encounter with your self that lays bare insecurities, fears, and doubts. This pursuit is as much about peeling away layers of ego as it is about elevating the spirit, a delicate balance that requires courage in the face of uncertainty. Here is where the guidance of a spiritual teacher is a treasure. A teacher has the wisdom to offer gentle prompting or a firm shove when needed to traverse less-traveled paths. In doing so, they remind us to cherish our imperfections and find peace in the continuous act of becoming.

I began studying Sikhism and Kundalini Yoga under the guidance of Yogi Bhajan when I was 19 years old. I longed to walk a spiritual path, but I knew *literally* nothing about anything. I will never know why he accepted me as a student, but he did, and I stayed with him until his passing in 2004. During these 30 years, I got married, had a child, and advanced my professional career. Together, my family and I lived near a 3HO ashram, where we still reside today. The teachings in this small book are all from Yogi Bhajan, and he never let up stressing the importance of a consistent sadhana above all else.

Yogi Bhajan in 2019.

A spiritual teacher is a treasure in today's environment, where the converging streams of technology and tradition create a complex web of motivations and practices. They are the translators of age-old wisdom into the lingua franca of contemporary seekers. Their intuition and experience scaffold the ancient practices, making them accessible and relevant today.

FINDING A SPIRITUAL TEACHER

Embarking on the quest to find the right teacher is an intensely personal process. It demands a frank, introspective look into the very core of your values and spiritual yearnings. A teacher who aligns harmoniously with your innate beliefs can offer insights that resonate deeply within you, echoing the core of who you are.

In traditional spiritual disciplines, it is said that when the seeker is ready, the teacher appears. Finding a teacher is not a matter of external search but an inner readiness. But how do you know when you've found the teacher who is right for you? The Buddha himself gave the most profound guidance I know on this topic, known as *The Four Reliances of the Buddha.*

The Four Reliances (*Catuḥpratisaraṇa* in Sanskrit) are guidelines taught in Mahayana Buddhism to help practitioners discern the true Dharma.

They encourage students to look beyond superficial appearances and cultivate inner wisdom. Here are the Four Reliances:

1. *One should not rely on the individual, but on the Dharma.* – Do not become attached to the teacher's personality or charisma. Rely instead on the truth of their teachings. Even if the teacher is flawed, the Dharma is still pure.
2. *One should not rely on the words, but on the meaning.* – A teacher may express wisdom in many forms. Don't cling to literal interpretations. Seek the deeper meaning, which may transcend language or cultural framing.
3. *One should not rely on the provisional meaning, but on the definitive meaning.* - Some teachers are skillful in tailoring wisdom for specific times or audiences. Learn to distinguish the ultimate truth from relative teachings, and focus on the former.
4. *One should not rely on ordinary consciousness, but on wisdom.* – True understanding arises through meditation and direct experience, not intellectual analysis alone. Find a guide who teaches from their inner realization.[i]

Relying on the Teacher Within

Every day when I begin my sadhana, it is with the prayer *"Ong Namo Gurudev Namo"* – I bow to the eternal, creative consciousness, I bow to my Gurudev. So, you must ask yourself, who is your Gurudev? Who is the one who brings you out of the darkness of the spirit?

You may not know the answer to that right now, but we all have a gurudev who guides us, and you will discover this through your sadhana journey. You don't need to rush to name your gurudev – it is a force that is there and working with you even now. In time, your gurudev will reveal themselves to you, often when you least expect it. Your job is to be ready for when the time comes.

In Sikhism, the concept of Guru extends beyond the physical realm. Although the ten Sikh Gurus lived in human form, their words and wisdom were compiled into the Siri Guru Granth Sahib, along with other enlightened saints of the time. The 10th Guru, Guru Gobind Singh Ji, instructed the Sikhs to regard the Siri Guru Granth Sahib as their eternal Guru and guide. The Guru is not the ink and pages of the book, although we give this the highest reverence, but the *Shabad*, the sacred sound current that connects the seeker to the Divine. The Shabad is more than scripture or poetry; it is a living frequency of Truth.

This is the *Shabad Guru*, the Gurudev of every Sikh and the heart of sadhana in the Sikh tradition. It is the subtle, formless teacher that lives as sound, vibration, and meaning. Through deep listening (*suniai*) and loving repetition (*jap*), the practitioner awakens to Divine Consciousness; not through devotion to a person, but through immersion in the eternal Word.

———

12

DEEPENING YOUR SADHANA PRACTICE

There comes a time in every sadhak's journey when you begin to sense a dimension of existence that is subtle, unseen, yet profoundly real; one that permeates all that is. This is an exciting phase, and one where you long to push forward in your practice. This is a natural sign that your spiritual discipline is maturing, and you are being invited into a more profound dimension of experience.

To deepen your sadhana is to step beyond routine into the sacred unknown. This may take the form of expanding your sadhana to include advanced kriyas that engage subtle energies and stabilize the consciousness in a higher state of awareness. It may involve participating in group sadhana, where the collective vibration amplifies everyone's intention. Or perhaps committing to an extended *japa* practice—the devotional repetition of a mantra with focused reverence over 1,100 or even 11,000 repetitions. Some are drawn to immerse themselves in silent retreats, where extended periods of inner stillness reveal new layers of the self. Others feel called to spiritual travel or pilgrimage, walking the ancient paths of saints and sages in India, Tibet, or beyond, allowing sacred geography to catalyze inner awakening. Each avenue deepens your relationship with the Divine and reorients your life toward your purpose.

By now, you have established a steady sadhana, balanced with devotion, meditation, and gratitude, within a time frame that suits your life and circumstances. Expanding your current practice is a simple process when your heart calls for more. To begin with, extend the invocation part of your sadhana. Read the full Japji Sahib or a prayer from your tradition. If you are already reciting the Japji Sahib, then add on the *Jap Sahib* - the *bani,* or sacred writings, of Guru Gobind Singh. For the Sikhs, we recite five banis in the morning, a goal you can work towards. By extending your devotional efforts first, you lay out a smooth path and lessen the pitfalls of ego.

EXPLORING ADVANCED KRIYAS

Exploring advanced kriyas and pranayama techniques can enrich your sadhana. These practices offer a deeper experience of the subtle energies within, enhancing both your sadhana's physical and spiritual aspects. Advanced kriyas—dynamic movements combined with breathwork—awaken dormant energies and clear energetic blockages. Engaging with these practices requires a degree of mastery over foundational techniques, ensuring that your body and mind are prepared for the intensity they bring.

Resources such as books and online instructions from 3HO or the Kundalini Research Institute provide a comprehensive guide for those ready to explore advanced practices. These materials offer detailed explanations and demonstrations, making intricate techniques accessible to those seeking to deepen their understanding and enhance their practice.

In-person workshops and meditation intensives also provide invaluable immersion opportunities. These settings allow you to learn directly from experienced teachers who can offer personalized guidance and adjustments that enable you to explore the nuances of advanced techniques with confidence.

Exploring advanced techniques is not just about adding complexity; it's about enriching your practice with depth and intention. As you engage with advanced kriyas, you'll discover new layers of consciousness and spiritual insight. It is an opportunity to challenge yourself while nurturing the connection between mind, body, and spirit, an invitation to fully embrace sadhana's transformative power.

When you explore advanced kriyas, you embark on a path of growth that requires commitment and an open mind. With each breath, you will deepen your understanding of self and spirit.

BENEFITS OF GROUP SADHANA AND MEDITATION

Meditating with others in a group is a means to deepen your spiritual practice and experience the transformative power of collective meditation. Group sadhana enhances group consciousness, allowing individual energies to harmonize and elevate the experience. This collective practice amplifies the impact of meditation, fostering a sense of unity and shared purpose among participants. It may not be something you can do every day, but it's an experience I encourage you to explore.

The power of group meditation lies in its ability to transform individual efforts into something greater than the sum of its parts. As you contribute your unique energy to the group, you'll find that the shared journey enriches your own, offering insights and connections that might remain hidden in solitary practice.

Group meditation experiences can be found in almost every religious tradition.

1. Your local Sikh Gurdwara will hold a Sunday morning service open to all. Please come with your head covered (both men and women) and be prepared to remove your shoes and socks before sitting on the floor. *Ragis,* spiritual musicians, sing Gurbani Kirtan while the sangat listens in meditation.
2. Your local Kundalini Yoga teacher will either host or know how to participate in group Aquarian Sadhana. You can find a teacher through the International Kundalini Yoga Teachers Association (https://www.ikyt.org) or the Yoga Alliance Directory (https://www.yogaalliance.org). If none are nearby, you can always join an online group sadhana.

3. In most areas, Buddhist *sanghas* (spiritual communities of practitioners) are readily available for those seeking support in mindfulness meditation. These gatherings are often held in meditation centers or temples. I have always found Buddhist groups welcoming to newcomers and offering teachings rooted in ancient wisdom that are still relevant to modern life.

4. Christian group prayer and study gatherings are widely available in most communities, offering spaces for fellowship, spiritual reflection, and deepening one's relationship with God. These groups often meet in churches, homes, or online, and may focus on Bible study, shared prayer, contemplation, or service.

SPIRITUAL TRAVEL, INTENSIVES, AND RETREATS

Visiting historical temples and monasteries can profoundly shift your perspective on meditation. These places, steeped in spiritual energy, nurture introspection and growth. Whether it's the serenity of a Buddhist monastery nestled in the mountains, the vibrant intensity of a Hindu ashram, or Gregorian chanting in an old cathedral, these sites offer a unique opportunity to deepen your practice by immersing yourself in diverse spiritual cultures. This exposure broadens your understanding and enriches your spiritual journey.

Spiritual retreats provide an immersive experience that's hard to replicate in everyday life. The structured environment of a retreat offers intensive practice and guidance that accelerates personal growth. In a serene setting, you can explore new dimensions of meditation, free from the demands of your daily routine. The quietude and support foster an environment where profound insights often emerge, and sadhana takes on new depth and meaning.

Choosing the right retreat involves careful consideration and a little investigation. Not all retreats will resonate with you, so it's worth researching. Look into the reputation and experience of the leaders and the suitability of the locations. Understanding the structure and expectations of the program can help ensure the retreat aligns with your goals.

Some intensives may focus on silence, while others incorporate teachings to enhance practice. Knowing what to expect allows you to engage fully with the experience and maximize the benefits.

Japa intensive led by Jugat Guru Singh Khalsa in Mexico.

My preferred intensive experience is *japa*, or repetitive mantra chanting. In a japa intensive, the shared repetition amplifies the energy of the mantra, fostering a deep level of concentration. The vibrations produced by chanting a mantra 11,000 times have a tangible effect, harmonizing the group's energy and elevating the collective consciousness. There are several japa intensives hosted around the world, and I encourage you to try one. Check out the endnotes for links to Jugat Guru Singh's intensives.[i]

In these spaces, whether traveling to distant lands or gathering close to home, an opening emerges; a chance to grow beyond perceived limitations and explore untapped potential within. Spiritual travel and retreats are more than just adventures; they are invitations to step into a world where transformation awaits in every breath.

13

THE LIFELONG PATH OF
SADHANA

As you continue with sadhana, you realize it is a lifelong commitment to personal and spiritual evolution. This path invites continuous growth, where each day offers a new opportunity for deeper understanding.

Embracing a path of learning means remaining open to adaptation, allowing your practice to transform as you do. Meditation practice is not static; it deepens and changes with experience. Over time, you may find yourself drawn to different techniques or exploring new traditions that resonate with your current life stage. What began as a simple breath-focused meditation might evolve into more complex practices as your understanding and capacity grow. This natural evolution reflects your journey and the unfolding of your inner world. As life shifts, so does your engagement with meditation, ensuring it remains a meaningful part of your daily life.

A commitment to spiritual growth involves continually seeking new challenges and experiences that push your boundaries. Regular self-assessment helps you identify areas for development and refines your practice. Be curious enough to seek out teachings or intensives that expand your horizons. This commitment involves courage, stepping beyond your comfort zone to explore uncharted territories within yourself. By nurturing this spirit of exploration, you ensure that your sadhana remains vibrant and transformative.

Sadhana is the art of living with awareness and purpose, not just sitting in meditation. This approach invites a shift from reactivity to responsiveness. The awareness cultivated in sadhana becomes a faculty that accompanies every act, whether speaking, eating, working, or resting. Ordinary routines, once viewed as distractions, become points of spontaneous spiritual practice. Through consistent application, the inner life and outer life come into balance.

Sadhana also deepens our resilience. It strengthens the ability to remain calm and steady in fluctuating conditions. This does not mean avoiding difficulty but learning to meet it without being consumed. A consistent sadhana offers tools for maintaining equilibrium during stress and uncertainty.

Devotion to a spiritual ideal, whether a teacher, a divine principle, or a sacred word, further strengthens one's orientation. In the Sikh tradition, for instance, the remembrance of the Guru's wisdom offers clarity and moral direction. For others, devotion may be silent prayer, mantra, or inner dialogue. What matters is opening your heart to the experience of something sacred.

The path ahead is yours to shape, filled with opportunities for growth, learning, and profound transformation.

CONCLUSION

As we reach the end of our shared journey through the pages of this book, let's take a moment to reflect on the path we've traveled together. We have explored the many facets of sadhana, from the gentle art of setting up a dedicated sadhana space to embracing a consistent routine that includes meditation. We've delved into the core meditation techniques that form a sadhana and integrated these practices into the rhythm of daily life. We've examined the benefits of a consistent sadhana and addressed common challenges, such as motivation, doubt, and mental chatter, those pesky companions that sometimes divert us from our goals.

The journey we've embarked upon is not just about learning techniques; it is about opening doors to profound personal and spiritual growth. It's a journey that invites you to shed layers that no longer serve you and embrace the person you are.

I hope you've discovered that sadhana is incredibly inclusive and accessible. Regardless of your background or previous experience with meditation, this practice welcomes you. We've incorporated perspectives from various religious and cultural traditions, ensuring that sadhana is a practice for everyone, whether you're a beginner finding your footing or a seasoned meditator seeking to deepen your experience.

One of the key messages is the importance of personalizing your practice. Sadhana is not a rigid set of rules but a flexible framework that adapts to your unique needs and lifestyle. Experiment with different techniques, find a schedule that suits you, and allow your sadhana to evolve as you do. Remember, there is no right or wrong way to engage with sadhana—only the way that feels most authentic to you.

As you continue your path, embrace sadhana as a lifelong journey of self-discovery and spiritual development. It offers endless possibilities for growth and fulfillment. Each day, you can deepen your connection to yourself and the world, living with intention and purpose.

I encourage you to commit to your daily meditation practice with enthusiasm and dedication. As you journey inward, remember the power of community. Share your experiences and insights with others and foster a supportive circle of friends who share your passion for sadhana.

Before we part ways, I want to express my heartfelt gratitude for joining me on this journey. Your willingness to explore and embrace sadhana is a gift to yourself and the world. I am honored to have shared these pages with you, and I look forward to hearing about how sadhana enriches your life.

May your journey be filled with peace, power, and presence. Thank you for allowing me to be a part of it.

———

EPILOGUE: THE REASON I LOVE MY SADHANA
A PERSONAL NOTE

Sadhana is a devotional offering in the quiet pre-dawn hours, when my soul bows before the Infinite. In that silence, the boundaries of ordinary life soften, and I glimpse into expanded realities that dissolve any frustration or restlessness I may carry. It is a sacred space where I can send love and prayers of protection to those I cherish, including souls who have already passed beyond this world. Each day, sadhana feels like a step deeper into the presence of spirit, where I grow in awareness and feel the nearness of my Guru, guiding me with quiet grace.

I am so grateful for the Sikh path—its history, its traditions, its rituals, and its discipline. It is a container that safely holds my heart in this ever-changing world. I find comfort in walking a path shaped by those who came before, in knowing I am part of an unbroken lineage of simple seekers, holy saints, and great warriors. I love that the Sikh tradition revolves around the *Naam*, the sacred sound current, the primal vibration that is the pulse of universal consciousness. My sadhana is a celebration of this sound current, vibrating through my tongue, resonating in my ears, and echoing in the chambers of my heart. Naam stretches across the fabric of the cosmos, flowing in the space between the stars and penetrating the space within my atoms.

I lay my head at the feet of Guru Gobind Singh. He is with me, not as a memory or imagination but as a living radiance, timeless, subtle, and ever near. He offers his hand freely to those who choose to walk his path, welcoming us not only as devotees but as his beloved sons and daughters. To attune to his essence is to encounter a warrior of the purest kind—one who fought not for conquest, but for Dharma, for the freedom of all to worship the Divine in their own way. His sword was lifted only in defense, never in aggression. I am his daughter. Once you have this experience, you can never deny it.

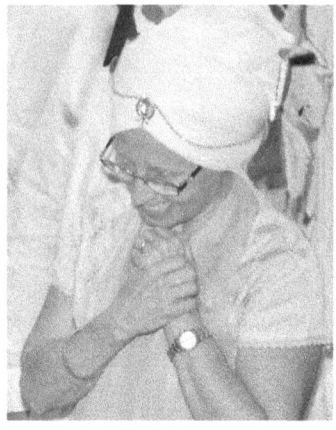

Beyond that, I am no one special. My ancestors were sailing Viking ships and still fighting with clubs when India was birthing a consciousness revolution that changed the world. And yet, even as a foreign stranger, Guru Gobind Singh welcomed me as his spiritual daughter. He opened my heart, altered the course of my life, and infused every part of it with meaning and depth. He is woven into my life, strengthening and illuminating me from within. I will forever be grateful to Yogi Bhajan for his wisdom and guidance, bringing me to the feet of Guru Gobind Singh.

———

APPENDIX 1. WHO ARE THE SIKHS

I have frequently referenced Sikhs and Sikhism throughout this book. Although it is the fifth-largest world religion with 25 million adherents worldwide, many people in the West are unfamiliar with it. I want to share a bit about it here for those who are interested in learning more.

Sikhism is a monotheistic religious tradition that originated in the Punjab region of South Asia in the 15th century. It was founded by Guru Nanak Dev Ji (1469–1539) and developed through the lives and teachings of nine human Gurus who succeeded him. The Sikh path integrates contemplative devotion, ethical living, social equality, and spiritual sovereignty. While its origins are situated in the fertile cultural and religious landscape of Punjab, where Hinduism, Islam, and Sufi mysticism coexisted, it evolved into a spiritual path with unique theological foundations and a clearly defined religious identity.

The Sikh worldview centers on the direct experience of the Divine, who is both immanent and transcendent, without form, name, or gender. Sikhs believe in one Creator, known by many names. This Sacred Essence is realized through meditation on the Divine Name (*Naam*), service (*seva*), and the grace of the Guru (*gurprasad*). The Sikh community, or *Panth*, continues to evolve under the guidance of the *Siri Guru Granth Sahib*, the sacred scripture.

HISTORICAL ORIGINS

Guru Nanak was born in 1469 in Talwandi (now Nankana Sahib, Pakistan), during a period of profound political, religious, and cultural upheaval. His enlightenment experience, expressed in the declaration *Na ko Hindu, Na ko Musalman* ("there is no Hindu, there is no Muslim"), signified not a denial of religious practice but a call to transcend sectarian identities in pursuit of the One Divine Reality.

Nanak's revelation led to the founding of a spiritual path that rejected caste, ritualism, chauvinism, and religious exclusivity. He traveled extensively on foot throughout South Asia, the Middle East, and Eastern Europe, engaging in dialogue with mystics, ascetics, and theologians, proclaiming the message of *Ik Ongkaar*—One Universal Creator—through song and verse.

CORE THEOLOGICAL BELIEFS

Sikh theology is outlined concisely in the *Mul Mantra*, the opening verse of the Siri Guru Granth Sahib:

> *One Universal Creator. Truth is His Name. Creative Being Personified. No Fear. No Hatred. The Image of the Undying One, Beyond Birth, Self-Existent. By Guru's Grace Chant and Meditate!*
>
> *True in the Primal Beginning. True Throughout the Ages. True Here and Now. O Nanak, Forever and Ever True.*

This verse serves as the ontological foundation of Sikhism. The Divine is not separate from the world but permeates it; creation itself is a manifestation of the Formless One. The soul seeks union with the Divine through humility, love, and meditation.

THE SIRI GURU GRANTH SAHIB

The Siri Guru Granth Sahib is the central scripture and eternal Guru of the Sikhs. It was compiled by Guru Arjan Dev, the 5th Guru, in 1604 and later sanctified by Guru Gobind Singh, the 10th Guru, in 1708 as the final Guru. It contains 1,430 pages of spiritual verse in *Gurmukhi* script, composed in multiple languages and musical *raag*. The Guru of the Sikhs is not merely a book—the pages, the ink, or the digital code on a screen—but the eternal Truth embedded within its teachings. This Truth is accessed through devotion, humility, and meditative awareness. The Siri Guru Granth Sahib is the living Guru of the Sikhs and is given the ultimate devotion and respect. When you come into a Sikh *Gurdwara* (temple), the congregation bows to the Siri Guru Granth Sahib upon entering.

The Siri Guru Granth Sahib Ji, the living Guru of the Sikhs.

The Granth includes the hymns of the Sikh Gurus and those of Hindu and Muslim mystics such as Bhagat Kabir, Farid, Namdev, and Ravidas —verses selected for their devotional and enlightened messages. The *Shabad*, or divine Word, is considered the True Guru. Reading or singing *Gurbani*, the verses of the Siri Guru Granth Sahib, is not merely an intellectual or musical exercise but a spiritual communion.

THE KHALSA AND SIKH IDENTITY

Guru Gobind Singh, the 10th Sikh Guru.

In 1699, Guru Gobind Singh initiated the *Khalsa*, a spiritual and martial order of committed Sikhs dedicated to upholding righteousness and divine sovereignty. Khalsa are distinct, wearing their bold turbans as a declaration of their commitment and integrity. The Khalsa are bound to observe the *Panj Kakaar* - the Five Ks:

1. **Kesh** – Uncut hair, honoring the perfection of the creation in its natural state.
2. **Kanga** – Wooden comb, to keep the hair untangled and represent the importance of cleanliness inside and out.
3. **Kara** – Steel bracelet, a constant reminder to act with honor,

encircling the wrist as an unbreakable bond with righteousness.

4. **Kachera** – Cotton undergarments, representing chastity, modesty, and moral strength.
5. **Kirpan** –Sword or dagger worn to demonstrate the Khalsa commitment to justice and defense of the weak and oppressed.

These are not symbols, but sacred commitments that reflect inner discipline and readiness to serve. From its inception, Sikhism has carried a political dimension rooted in upholding justice. The ideal of the *Sant-Sipahi* (Saint-Soldier) captures the Khalsa spirit: one who embodies divine love and defends righteousness with unbounded courage.

THE SIKHS TODAY

Today, Sikhs reside all over the world, with significant populations in India, the United Kingdom, Canada, and the United States. While many Sikhs are baptized members of the Khalsa, others identify as cultural or philosophical adherents of Sikh values.

Gurdwaras serve as spiritual and community centers, offering *langar* (food served equally to all, in the Name of the Guru), educational services, and spiritual gatherings. Sikhism remains a living tradition that honors its sacred history while engaging with the challenges of the modern world. To be a Sikh is to walk the seeker's path: to live with humility, speak with truth, act with justice, and remember the Divine in every breath. It is not only a religion, but a discipline of consciousness; a merging of mystic experience and ethical living. Through the grace of the Guru, the Sikh aspires not only to realize the Divine but to manifest that realization in service to the world.

APPENDIX 2. PRANAYAMA FOR YOUR SADHANA

Beginning your sadhana with pranayama prepares the body and mind for deep meditation. Pranayama is essential for awakening the kundalini energy within the body and regulating subtle energies.

Pranayama is an ancient yogic discipline that originated within the Vedic tradition and was systematized in later yogic and philosophical texts. The earliest seeds of pranayama are found in the Rig Veda and Upanishads, where breath (prana) is revered as a life-sustaining, cosmic force. Later, in the Yoga Sutras of Patanjali (2nd century BCE), he identifies pranayama as the 4th limb of the eight-limbed yoga path.

Guru Nanak Dev ji tells us in the Slok at the conclusion of the Japji Sahib:

ਪਵਣੁ ਗੁਰੂ ਪਾਣੀ ਪਿਤਾ ਮਾਤਾ ਧਰਤਿ ਮਹਤੁ ॥

Pavan guru paanee pitaa maataa dharat mahat

The wind is my Teacher, water is my Father, and Earth is the Great Mother of all.

With these words, Guru Nanak evokes a sacred vision of the natural world as the primary spiritual family of humanity. *Pavan*—the wind, the breath, the moving air—is not merely a physical element but a divine presence that teaches, guides, and gives life. The breath becomes our Guru, a teacher that connects us to the infinite through its silent rhythm. It carries the prana, the vital life force, the subtle energy that sustains all living beings. When we become aware of the breath, we begin to attune ourselves to this living teacher within. In this way, pranayama is not simply a yogic technique; it is a sacred dialogue with the Teacher that resides in each inhale and exhale. To sit and meditate with the breath is to sit at the feet of the Guru. Therefore, integrating conscious breathing into your daily sadhana is not only beneficial for health, it is a devotional act, a way of aligning with the rhythm of the cosmos and receiving the wisdom of the elements themselves.

There are hundreds of pranayama techniques, but here are four classical ones from Yogi Bhajan's teachings to start your journey. Included is a kriya for each pranayama. You can practice the breathing techniques on their own or as part of a kriya.

———

LONG DEEP BREATHING

Long Deep Breathing is a fundamental technique in Kundalini Yoga that promotes relaxation and mental clarity. By consciously controlling the breath, practitioners can calm the mind, reduce stress, and prepare the body for meditation. This practice involves slow, deep inhalations and exhalations, engaging the full capacity of the lungs to enhance oxygen intake and circulation.

Instructions:

1. **Posture**: Sit comfortably, with a straight spine, shoulders relaxed.
2. **Breath**: Close your eyes and bring your attention to your breath.

- Inhalation - Inhale slowly and deeply through the nose, allowing the abdomen to expand first, followed by the chest.
- Exhalation- Exhale wholly and slowly through the nose, allowing the chest to relax first, followed by the abdomen.
- Establish a smooth and even rhythm, ensuring that the inhalation and exhalation are of equal length.

3. Continue this breathing pattern for 2 to 3 minutes, gradually increasing the duration as you become more comfortable with the practice.

Benefits of Long Deep Breathing:

- Promotes relaxation and reduces stress.
- Enhances oxygen intake and circulation.
- Balances the nervous system.
- Prepares the mind and body for meditation.

Incorporating Long Deep Breathing into your daily sadhana can serve as a powerful tool to center yourself and deepen your practice.

KRIYA - LONG BREATH TO BALANCE THE NERVOUS ENERGIES

From the book: *Praana, Praanee, Praanayam: Exploring the Breath Technology of Kundalini Yoga as Taught by Yogi Bhajan.*

This meditation helps to harmonize the nervous and glandular systems, balance the ego, and relieve stress in the shoulders.

Instructions:

1. **Posture:** Sit in a comfortable meditative position with a straight spine. With the elbows bent, raise the hands up and in until they meet at the level of the heart, a few inches from the body, palms facing the chest.
2. **Mudra:** Place the palm of the right hand against the back of the left hand. Hold the hands and forearms parallel to the ground so that the fingers of the right-hand point toward the left side and the

Posture and mudra for Long Breath.

   fingers of the left-hand point toward the right side. Press the thumb tips together.
3. **Eyes:** The eyes are nine-tenths closed.
4. **Breath:** Inhale deeply through the nose and calmly hold the breath in for 15-20 seconds. Exhale completely through your nose and hold your breath out for 15-20 seconds. Concentrate on the breath.

This meditation helps balance the entire nervous system and glandular system. By putting the thumbs together in the mudra, the sciatic nerve is neutralized at the point of ego. (Thumbs represent the energy of the ego.) This balance puts pressure on specific meridian points in the shoulders.

FOUR-STROKE BREATH

Four-stroke breath, also known as box or square breathing, is a simple yet powerful pranayama technique for calming the nervous system and improving focus. It involves equal-length phases of inhalation, breath retention, exhalation, and a second retention—each segment typically lasting about four seconds. This structured rhythm helps to regulate the autonomic nervous system, supporting emotional balance and cognitive clarity.

Box breathing is widely used in stress management and athletic training. Studies have shown that slow, rhythmic breathing practices like box breathing can reduce anxiety symptoms, lower blood pressure, and improve heart rate variability. It is used by professionals in high-stress environments, such as the US Navy SEALs, to maintain calm under pressure and enhance decision-making capabilities.

How to Practice 4-Stroke Breath:

1. Sit comfortably with a straight spine and relaxed shoulders.
2. Inhale slowly through the nose for a count of 4 seconds.
3. Hold the breath in for a count of 4 seconds.
4. Exhale gently through the nose for a count of 4 seconds.
5. Hold the breath out (lungs empty) for a count of 4 seconds.
6. Repeat this cycle for 2 to 5 minutes, gradually increasing duration as desired.

As you continue the practice, you may experience a deep sense of inner steadiness. The consistent rhythm promotes activation of the parasympathetic nervous system, your body's "rest and digest" state, enhancing physiological recovery and emotional resilience.

Benefits of 4-Stroke Breath

- Reduces stress and anxiety by activating the parasympathetic nervous system.
- Improves focus and mental clarity, especially under pressure.
- Lowers blood pressure and promotes cardiovascular balance.

KRIYA - FOUR-STROKE BREATH FOR REJUVENATION

From the book: *Praana, Praanee, Praanayam: Exploring the Breath Technology of Kundalini Yoga as Taught by Yogi Bhajan.*

This pranayama technique revitalizes the body and mind by stimulating the glandular system and enhancing overall vitality.

Posture and mudra for 4-stroke Breath Kriya.

Instructions:

1. **Posture**: Sit in a comfortable meditative position with a straight spine. Bring the hands together at the heart center. Keep the elbows near the sides of the ribs. Turn the palms up and open the hands, spreading the fingers with the thumbs away from each other.
2. **Mudra**: The hands are slightly cupped with the outer sides of the pinkie finger touching. Keep your hands relaxed.
3. **Eyes**: With the back and neck straight, look down at the tip of the nose, creating a slight pressure on the optic nerve.
4. **Breath**: Four-stroke breath:

- Inhale deeply and completely through the mouth, without whistling, in four equal strokes (approximately 4 seconds).
- Hold the breath in for a count of four.
- Exhale completely through the nose in four equal strokes, mentally chanting the mantra Sa Ta Na Ma—one syllable per stroke.
- Hold your breath out for a count of four.

Create a powerful, rhythmic breath and keep that rhythm. Begin with 5 minutes and gradually, as you develop the rhythm, timing, and evenness of the breath, work up to 11 minutes and beyond. The maximum practice time is 31 minutes.

Maintain a controlled rhythm throughout the kriya to prevent it from unbalancing your nervous system. After practicing this powerful kriya, give yourself plenty of time to rest and return to normal.

———

NADI SODHANA - ALTERNATE NOSTRIL BREATHING

Nadi Sodhana Pranayama, often translated as "alternate nostril breathing," is a foundational yogic practice that purifies and balances the *nadis*, the subtle energy channels through which prana flows in the body. According to yogic physiology, there are 72,000 nadis in the human body, however, three are considered primary: *Ida, Pingala*, and *Sushumna*. The Ida Nadi, associated with the left nostril, governs the parasympathetic nervous system and represents the right-brain hemisphere's lunar, cooling, introspective energy. The Pingala Nadi, connected to the right nostril, corresponds with the sympathetic nervous system and represents solar, warming, logic-directed energy of the left-brain hemisphere. The central channel, Sushumna, runs along the spine and becomes active only when Ida and Pingala are in balance, allowing the kundalini energy to rise through the Sushumna and spiritual awareness to deepen.

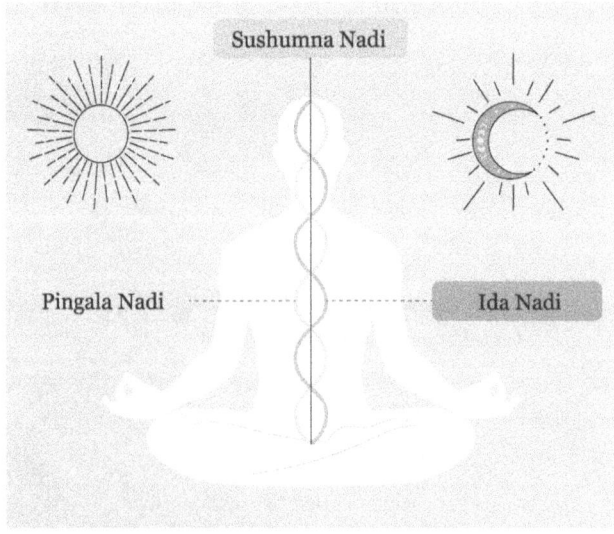

The literal meaning of Nadi Sodhana is "purification of the channels." By alternating the breath through each nostril in a slow rhythm, the practitioner balances the sympathetic and parasympathetic nervous systems, clears energetic blockages, and prepares the mind for deeper states of meditation. Scientific studies have confirmed the physiological benefits of alternate nostril breathing, including reduced anxiety, improved cardiovascular function, and enhanced cognitive performance (Saoji, Raghavendra, & Manjunath, 2019). In yogic terms, when the nadis are clear and balanced, the mind becomes calm, the breath flows freely, and the practitioner experiences heightened vitality and inner stillness—conditions conducive to higher states of consciousness.

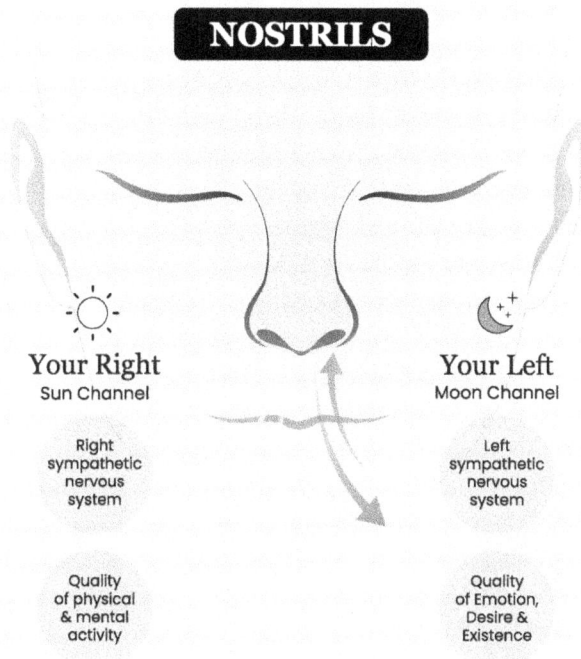

KRIYA - NADI CLEANSING WITH ALTERNATE NOSTRIL BREATHING

From the book: *Praana, Praanee, Praanayam: Exploring the Breath Technology of Kundalini Yoga as Taught by Yogi Bhajan.*

Instructions:

1. **Posture**: Sit in a comfortable, meditative position with a straight spine. Ensure that your stomach is empty or you have eaten only very lightly.
2. **Mudra**: Use your right hand to alternate the breath through the left and right nostrils. The tip of the thumb can block the right nostril, and either the index finger or the pinkie finger can block the left nostril. Apply only enough pressure to close the nostril gently and thoroughly.
3. **Breath**: Breath in this sequence:

Mudra and posture for Nadi Cleansing Kriya.

- Block off the right nostril and inhale deeply through the left nostril for a count of one.
- Hold your breath for a count of four.
- Block off the left and exhale through the right nostril for a count of two.
- Then inhale through the right nostril for a count of one.
- Hold your breath for a count of four.
- Block off the right and exhale through the left nostril for a count of two.

Continue this breath pattern of *inhale left – exhale right; inhale right – exhale left* for 15-62 minutes.

BREATH OF FIRE

Breath of Fire, also known as *Kapalabhati* or *Ajani Pranayama*, is an energizing breathing technique rooted in Kundalini Yoga. This breath involves rapid, rhythmic breaths with equal emphasis on inhalation and exhalation, typically performed through the nose. The breath is powered by active contractions of the diaphragm and abdominal muscles, creating a bellows-like effect that energizes the body and clears the mind. Unlike hyperventilation, Breath of Fire is practiced with control, maintaining a balanced and rhythmic breath.

The benefits of Breath of Fire are both physiological and psychological. Regular practice can enhance respiratory function, increase lung capacity, and strengthen the diaphragm. It stimulates the nervous system, promoting mental clarity and focus. Additionally, this technique aids in detoxification by expelling carbon dioxide and other waste gases from the lungs, thereby purifying the blood. Practitioners often report experiencing heightened energy levels and a sense of invigoration after practicing.

However, it's important to approach Breath of Fire with caution. Individuals with respiratory issues, cardiovascular conditions, or who are pregnant should consult a healthcare professional before attempting this pranayama. Beginners are advised to start slowly, focusing on proper technique rather than speed, and gradually increase the duration as they develop comfort and proficiency.

Incorporating Breath of Fire into a regular meditation routine can be a powerful tool for enhancing overall well-being, energy, and vitality.

How to Practice Breath of Fire

In Breath of Fire, we use the navel point to actively control exhalation. The muscular control area for the navel point is about 1-2 inches below the belly button.

1. To exhale, pull in on the navel point. This contraction squeezes the lower abdomen and pushes the diaphragm

upward, compressing the lungs and forcefully expelling air from them.

2. To inhale, relax the pressure in the navel area, which allows the lungs to decompress. As the lungs decompress, air flows inward with a passive inhale.

3. The breath is through the nose, and the inhalation and exhalation are of equal duration.

4. The breath is powerful, rhythmic, and rapid – 2-3 breaths per second once you achieve proficiency.

Posture is important with Breath of Fire. It is essential that the spine is straight and the rib cage lifted so that the upper body's weight does not hamper the pulsing of the navel. The body should stay relatively still and relaxed – only the navel is working hard.

———

APPENDIX 3. YOGA AS PREPARATION FOR MEDITATION

Yoga is more than a physical exercise—it is a powerful tool for harmonizing the body, breath, and mind in preparation for meditation. As part of your sadhana, yoga awakens vital energy and loosens physical tension. The movements of yoga activate the circulation of prana, aligning the body's subtle systems so you can enter meditation in a state of openness and balance. It's a sacred warm-up that clears the pathways for inner stillness to arise naturally.

Physically, yoga stretches prepare the body to sit comfortably for extended periods. Rather than struggling with stiffness, you build a foundation of ease and steadiness. This readiness is not just for comfort, it creates the conditions for profound inward focus. Like tuning an instrument before a performance, yoga helps ensure your body, breath, and mind are in harmony, allowing the deeper symphony of meditation to unfold.

There are many traditions of yoga—Hatha, Ashtanga, Iyengar, Vinyasa, and others—all offering unique ways to prepare for spiritual practice. My own path is grounded in Kundalini Yoga as taught by Yogi Bhajan, and here you will find a foundational set ideal for beginners.

I have also included one of my favorites from the hatha yoga tradition-*Surya Namaskar*, or Sun Salutations. It's a flowing sequence that awakens the body, builds strength, and gently stretches the spine and legs, perfect for shaking off sleep and preventing leg numbness during extended meditation sessions. Whether you follow these sets or explore your own practice, yoga becomes a gateway: from movement into stillness; from breath into being.

———

SAT KRIYA

Sat Kriya is one of the most essential and powerful practices in Kundalini Yoga. Though simple in form, it works deeply on the physical, energetic, and mental levels. It is a complete kriya in itself; combining posture, breath, mantra, and mental focus into a single meditative discipline.

How to Practice Sat Kriya

1. **Posture:** Sit on your heels in *Vajrasan* (Rock Pose) with a straight spine. For support, beginners may place a cushion or rolled blanket under the ankles or between the heels and the sitting bones.

2. **Mudra:** Stretch your arms straight overhead, keeping your biceps close to your ears. Interlace all the fingers except the index fingers, which point straight up. Men cross their right thumb over their left; women cross their left thumb over their right.

Posture and Mudra for Sat Kriya.

3. **Mantra and Breath:** Chant the mantra *Sat Naam* in a steady rhythm:

- On *Sat*, pull the navel point inward towards the spine with force.
- On *Naam*, relax the belly and allow the sound to flow gently.
- The breath adjusts naturally to the rhythm of the mantra, about 2 seconds per breath.

4. **Eyes:** Keep your eyes closed and focus on the brow point.

5. Start with 3 minutes. Depending on your experience and capacity, you may build up to 11 or 31 minutes over time.

Always follow the kriya with rest. After practicing Sat Kriya, lie down in *Shavasana* (Corpse Pose) for at least the same duration as the practice. This step is essential for integrating the effects.

Benefits of Sat Kriya

- Stimulates and channels kundalini energy up the spine.
- Strengthens the digestive and reproductive systems.
- Balances and redirects sexual energy toward higher consciousness.
- Builds nervous system resilience and emotional stability.
- Expands the aura and magnetic field, offering a sense of protection.
- Promotes a calm, focused mind.

Yogi Bhajan often emphasized that Sat Kriya should be practiced with precision and respect. Even a few minutes a day can produce powerful changes. However, overexertion without proper rest and guidance can create an imbalance. The key is consistency and slowly building your endurance.

————

BASIC SPINAL ENERGY SERIES

This is a great warm-up for meditation. The series works systematically from the base of the spine to the top. All 26 vertebrae receive stimulation, and all the chakras receive a burst of energy. Repetitions are specified here as 26, but you can do up to 108 repetitions. As you perform the movements, you can incorporate the mantra *Sat Naam* by inhaling and mentally repeating *Sat,* exhaling and mentally repeating *Naam.*

Be very controlled and gentle with your back. If you have back problems or any back injury, do not do this set without first consulting with your doctor.

1. Spinal Flex in *Sahajasan*:

Sit in Sahajasan, or Easy Pose. Grab your ankles or shins with both hands and deeply inhale as you flex the spine forward and the shoulders back. On the exhale, flex the spine back, rounding the shoulders forward. Repeat this exercise 26 times, then rest for 1 minute.

Posture for spinal flex in Sahajasan.

Posture for spinal flex in Vajrasan.

2. Spinal Flex in Vajrasan:

Sit on your heels with your spine straight and your hands on your thighs. This is Vajrasan, or Rock Pose. Continue to flex the spine in this position, inhaling as you flex forward and exhaling as you flex back, rounding the shoulders. Repeat this exercise 26 times, then rest for 2 minutes.

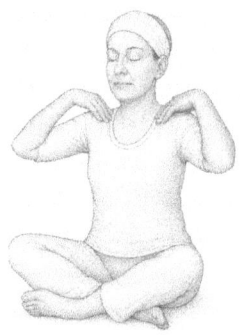

Hands on the shoulders, twist back and forth.

3. Spinal Twist:

Sit in Easy Pose and grasp the shoulders, with fingers in front and thumbs in back. Inhale and twist to the left, exhale and twist to the right. Try to maintain a pace of one inhale/exhale per second. Repeat 26 times. To end, inhale in the center, exhale, and relax. Rest for one minute.

―――――

4. Bear Grip at the Heart Center:

Lock the fingers in Bear Grip at the heart center. Move the elbows in a see-saw motion: Inhale right elbow up, left elbow down. Exhale right elbow down, left elbow up. Try to maintain a pace of one inhale and one exhale per second. Repeat 26 times. To conclude, inhale and pull as if trying to separate the hands. Exhale and relax.

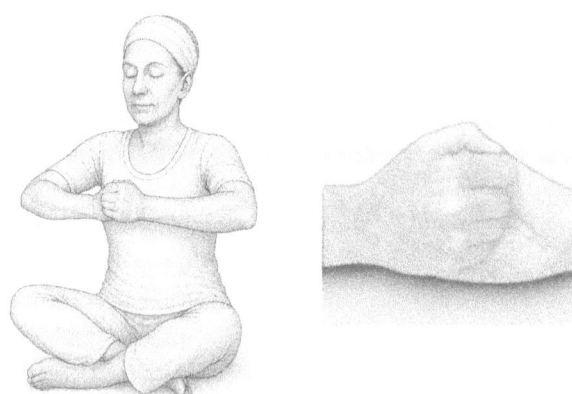

Hands in bear grip at the heart center.

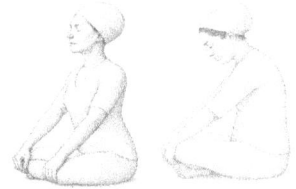

Hands grasping the knees, flex the upper spine.

5. Spinal Flex for Upper Spine:

While still in easy pose, grasp your knees firmly, keep your elbows straight, and flex the upper part of your spine. Inhale and arch forward, exhale and round the spine back. Repeat this exercise 26 times and rest for 1 minute.

———

6. Shoulder Shrugs: With the inhale, bring both shoulders up towards the ears and relax down with the exhale. Do this for a couple of minutes at a pace of more than one shrug per second. Inhale and hold the shoulders up for 15 seconds. Exhale and relax.

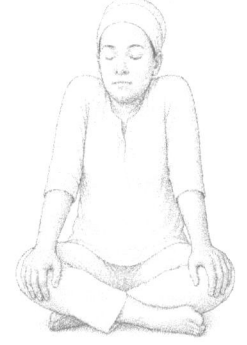

Shoulder Shrugs up and down.

———

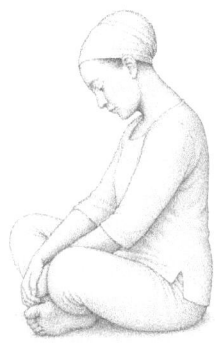

7. Neck rolls: Drop the chin to the chest and roll the head slowly 5 times to the left and 5 times to the right. Stretch the neck gently and avoid movement in any way that causes pain.

8. Bear Grip with Mulbandh:

Lock the fingers in Bear Grip at the level of the throat and pull with moderate strength. Inhale and hold the breath, apply *mulbandh*;* exhale and hold the breath out and apply mulbandh. Raise your arms above your head while maintaining a bear grip. Inhale and hold your breath, then apply mulbandh. Exhale and hold your breath out and apply mulbandh again. Repeat this complete cycle two more times.

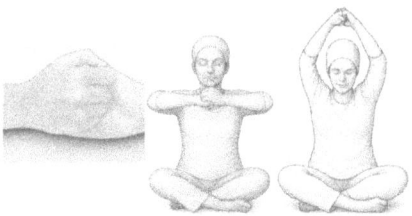

Bear grip at the throat with Mulbandh.

*Mulbandh is also known as "root lock". It is done with the simultaneous contraction of the navel point, the muscles of the pelvic floor, and the rectum. This *bandh*, or lock, stimulates the life-force energy in the lower chakras and elevates it.

———

Posture for Sat Kriya.

9. Sat Kriya:

Sit in Vajrasan and stretch your arms overhead for Sat Kriya. Continue for at least three minutes, then inhale and squeeze the body's muscles tightly, from the buttocks up the back and past the shoulders. Mentally allow the energy to flow through the top of the skull.

Relax: Lie on your back in corpse pose and completely relax for 15 minutes.

SURYA NAMASKAR - SUN SALUTATIONS

Each movement in Surya Namaskar is a prayer, a breath, and a gesture of reverence to the inner light. — T.K.V. Desikachar

Surya Namaskar, or Sun Salutation, is a foundational sequence in traditional hatha yoga that combines asana (physical postures) and breath in a dynamic, meditative flow. Rooted in Vedic sun worship and later codified in yoga systems such as those of the *Hatha Yoga Pradipika,* a 15th-century text by Swatmarama, Surya Namaskar is both a physical discipline and a devotional offering to *Surya,* the solar deity associated with consciousness, vitality, and illumination. Often practiced at sunrise, the sequence consists of twelve postures performed in a rhythmic cycle that mirrors the sun's arc across the sky.

Each movement is typically coordinated with a breath component in a smooth and uninterrupted flow—inhaling, exhaling, or retention. A complete cycle includes 12 movements.

Although I am including all 12 traditional postures here, modifying Surya Namaskar is not only acceptable—it is encouraged. A personalized approach fosters an evolving and lifelong relationship with this practice. You can adapt it to compensate for physical restrictions, low energy, and even limited time by adding, adjusting, or deleting asanas to extend or shorten the sequence as needed. Many more variations can be easily found on the internet, including more stretching, core strengthening, or any other focus you'd like to add. (I must confess that I sometimes adapt Surya Namaskar to avoid postures on the floor, so that my lovely dogs don't lick my face!)

Perform one movement per breath. If you need more time to stretch into the pose, take two breaths per pose. Using the breath in this way supports healing and calms the nervous system. Always prioritize breath over form, so that the entire set flows smoothly. If your breath becomes strained, slow down, stop, and rest. If you find the asana too challenging, an adjustment is noted for each posture to make it a little easier.

The 12 Postures of Surya Namaskar (Sun Salutation)

1. Pranamasana (Prayer Pose): Stand at the front edge of the mat with feet comfortably apart, equal weight on each foot, palms joined at the heart center. **Inhale/Exhale** with conscious attention until you are ready to move through the sequence.

———

2. Hasta Uttanasana (Raised Arms Pose):

As you **inhale**, raise your arms overhead, keeping them near your ears. Arch your head, arms, and upper back slightly, and lift your chest. With a deep inhale, stretch your spine from your heels to the tips of your fingers.

Adjustment: Diminish the arch if this creates strain in your lower back.

———

3. Padahastasana (Standing Forward Fold):

As you **exhale**, fold forward from the hips, bringing the palms to the floor beside the feet. Bring your head as close to your knees as possible, stretching your hamstrings as you exhale.

Adjustment: If you have trouble touching the floor, bend your knees slightly or use blocks under your hands.

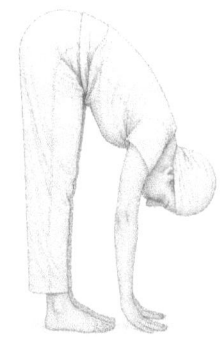

4. Ashwa Sanchalanasana (Low Lunge): As you **inhale**, step back with your right leg, drop your knee, lift your chest, and look forward. Try to keep the left foot between the hands. The top of the right foot is on the floor.

Adjustment: Replace with a standing lunge.

———

5. Dandasana (Plank Pose): While **exhaling**, step the left foot back to join the right, come up on the toes, and form a line from head to heels.

Adjustment: Drop the knees to table-top pose if core strength is limited.

———

6. Ashtangasana (8-Limbed Pose):

With the breath out, lower your knees, chest, and chin to the floor, raising your hips slightly.

Adjustment: Lower yourself slowly to the floor.

———

7. Bhujangasana (Cobra Pose):

As you **inhale**, slide your chest forward and lift into a gentle backbend. Keep your shoulders down from your ears, your hip bones on the floor, and your eyes towards the ceiling. Only rise as much as is comfortable.

8. Parvatasana (Downward-Facing Dog):

As you exhale, tuck the toes and lift the hips up and back, forming an inverted "V" shape. Stretch your arms straight and keep your heels on the floor. Gently stretch the backs of your legs.

Adjustment: Lift your heels or bend the knees to lighten the stretch.

———

9. Ashwa Sanchalanasana (Low Lunge – Left Leg Back):

As you **inhale**, step the right leg forward, extend the left leg back, and drop the knee, putting the top of the left foot on the floor. Lift the chest and look forward. Try to keep the right foot between the knees.

Adjustment: Use a standing lunge

———

10. Padahastasana (Standing Forward Fold):

*A*s you **exhale**, fold forward from the hips, bringing the palms to the floor beside the feet. Bring the head as close to the knees as you can.

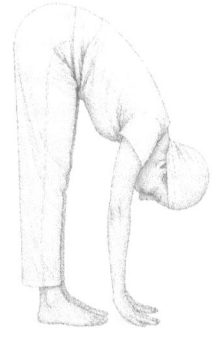

Adjustment: If you have trouble touching the floor, bend your knees or use blocks under your hands.

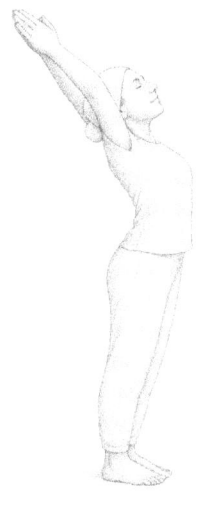

11.Hasta Uttanasana (Raised Arms Pose):

As you **inhale**, raise your arms overhead, keeping them near your ears. Arch your head, arms, and upper back slightly, and lift your chest. With a deep inhale, stretch your spine from your heels to the tips of your fingers.

Adjustment: Diminish the arch if this creates strain in your lower back.

---

12. Pranamasana (Prayer Pose):

Exhale as you stand once again at the front edge of the mat with feet comfortably apart, equal weight on each foot, palms joined at the heart center.

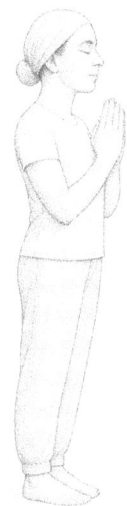

This completes the cycle of Sun Salutations. Do 2-3 sequences or more. On special days, such as the Summer or Winter Solstices, try completing 11 or 26 cycles.

APPENDIX 4. MANTRA AND MEDITATION

Laya Yoga, the yogic path of mantra meditation, is the sacred discipline of dissolving individual consciousness into the Universal Consciousness through the power of sound. In this tradition, mantra is not simply the repetition of words; it is a vibrational key that quiets the thinking mind and opens the inner space to profound spiritual insight.

Through steady and conscious repetition, mantra helps still the mind's habitual restlessness. As the sound current flows with intention, it harmonizes the body's subtle energies and draws focus inward. This process leads the practitioner beyond surface thought into a state of meditative absorption.

As written by Lama Zopa Rinpoche in *The Power of Mantra*:

> *Thinking of mantras as just some Sanskrit sounds to be chanted is an extremely limited view of what they are; they are much more than that. The sound of a mantra has the power to protect us, holding our mind from non-virtuous thoughts and fostering virtuous ones, thus allowing us to develop towards enlightenment.*

Each mantra carries a specific vibrational pattern, designed to penetrate the egoic structures of the psyche and guide consciousness back to its original, undifferentiated state. Over time, this becomes a journey of refinement, where emotional turbulence settles, clarity awakens, and the personal self begins to merge with the formless Absolute.

Chanting a mantra in sadhana is both the teacher and the path. Over time, it becomes a gateway to transformation, aligning the heart, mind, and soul with the deeper currents of truth.

The following are four mantras from the Sikh tradition, as taught by Yogi Bhajan. These are a good place to start, but you will find there are many, many more. I encourage you to find the one that resonates with you and explore its gifts in depth. A wise man once told me,

It's not about mastering countless mantras—what matters is deeply experiencing even one.

———

MUL MANTRA

The *Mul Mantra* (also spelled *Mool Mantra*, meaning "Root Mantra") is the foundational statement of Sikh philosophy as revealed by Guru Nanak Dev Ji. It appears at the beginning of the Japji Sahib, which is the beginning of the Siri Guru Granth Sahib, and is considered the essence of Sikh spiritual understanding.

Guru Nanak Dev Ji, the first Sikh Guru and founder of Sikhism, exhibited a contemplative nature and a profound spiritual sensitivity from a very young age. Though raised in a Hindu family, Guru Nanak questioned the rigid rituals and social divisions he saw around him, including the caste system and the separation of people by religion. His early encounters with Hindu and Muslim teachers shaped his understanding, but he consistently sought the more profound truth beyond the confines of religious rituals.

A pivotal moment in Guru Nanak's life occurred around the age of 30, when he disappeared while bathing in the Kali Bein river. For three days, he was missing, and it was believed he had drowned. However, when he reappeared, he remained silent for some time, then began teaching the Oneness of the Divine Spirit throughout the world.

Guru Nanak had experienced a profound spiritual revelation during those three days: a direct vision of the Oneness of all creation and the Divine presence permeating everything. From then on, he dedicated his life to spreading a message of universal love, devotion to the One, honest living, and service to humanity. He traveled extensively, composing hymns that would later become part of the Siri Guru Granth Sahib, and planting the seeds of a path that would offer liberation through remembrance of the Divine Name and compassionate action.

Guru Nanak Dev Ji, the 1st Guru of the Sikhs.

The Mul Mantra, Guru Nanak's greatest bani, is both a profound philosophical summary of the nature of the Divine and a sacred meditative formula. It affirms the unity of all existence and describes the timeless, formless essence of the Creator. For Sikhs, it serves as a daily affirmation and spiritual compass, guiding the seeker inward. More than a prayer, the Mul Mantra is a direct revelation of Truth—its devoted repetition aligns the practitioner with divine attributes, awakening and transforming both inner consciousness and outer life.

Here is a translation of the mantra:

ੴ	Ik Ong Kar	One Universal Creator
ਸਤਿ ਨਾਮੁ	Sat Naam	Your Name is Truth
ਕਰਤਾ ਪੁਰਖੁ	Kartaa Purakh	Creator Personified
ਨਿਰਭਉ ਨਿਰਵੈਰੁ	Nirbhau Nirvair	Without Fear, Without Hatred
ਅਕਾਲ ਮੂਰਤਿ	Akaal Moorat	The Image of the Undying One
ਅਜੂਨੀ ਸੈਭੰ	Ajoonee Saibhang	Beyond Birth, Self Existent
ਗੁਰ ਪ੍ਰਸਾਦਿ	Gur Prasaad	By the Guru's Grace
ਜਪੁ	Jaap	Chant and Meditate!
ਆਦਿ ਸਚੁ	Aad Sach	True in the Primal Beginning
ਜੁਗਾਦਿ ਸਚੁ	Jugaad Sach	True Throughout the Ages
ਹੈ ਭੀ ਸਚੁ	Hai Bhee Sach	True Here and Now
ਨਾਨਕ ਹੋਸੀ ਭੀ ਸਚੁ	Nanak Hosee Bhee Sach	O Nanak, Forever True.

How to Chant the Mul Mantra

The easiest way to chant the Mul Mantra is to do it along with a recording, so that you learn the pronunciation and rhythm of the verse. Many beautiful musical varieties exist on all streaming platforms. Try artists such as Snatam Kaur, Gurunam Singh, or White Sun. If you prefer the non-music versions, you will find many on YouTube.

When exploring different recordings of the Mul Mantra, you may notice variations in where it ends. Some scholars hold that it concludes with the words "Gur Prasaad," viewing this as the culmination of the theological root. Many others believe the complete mantra continues through "Nanak Hosee Bhee Sach." These final lines affirm that Truth is eternal through all ages and essential to the message.

Start with a short meditation and read the words as you chant along with the recording. Before long, you will know them by heart and easily sit with eyes closed, meditating while you recite. Extend the time for as long as you are comfortable, as there is no limit on how long you can meditate on this divine mantra.

MORNING CALL – EK ONG KAAR, SAT NAAM, SIRI WAHE GURU

One of the most potent and foundational mantras in Kundalini Yoga, as taught by Yogi Bhajan, is known as the *Morning Call*, or *Long Ek Ong Kaar*.

In the early 1970s, when the 3HO movement was young, this mantra was chanted for 2.5 hours every morning in group sadhana. It was my introduction to sadhana, and the growth of consciousness it opened in me, I cannot describe. For this, I will always be grateful. It is still chanted today for 7 minutes in Aquarian Sadhana at 3HO ashrams and events around the world.

Yogi Bhajan introduced this mantra to the West in 1969, referring to it as the key to unlocking the chakras and fostering deep meditative awareness. Though not found in the exact phrasing within classical Sikh scripture, its components are a familiar part of Sikh bani. The words mean:

Ek Ong Kaar – There is One Creator

Sat Naam – Truth is the identity

Siri Wahe Guru – Great is the indescribable Guru

Together, this mantra affirms the unity of all existence (*Ek Ong Kaar*), aligns the self with the vibration of Truth (*Sat Naam*), and expresses ecstatic awe at the Infinite guiding force (*Wahe Guru*).

———

How to Practice Long Ek Ong Kaar

Traditionally, Morning Call is chanted in a prolonged form, with each sound articulated clearly and with deep breath control.

1. **Posture**: Sit in Sahajasan, Easy Pose, with the chin tucked and the neck very straight - Jalandhar Bundh.
2. **Mudra**: Have the hands in *Gyan Mudra,* the thumb touching the pad of the forefinger, on the knees or resting comfortably in the lap.
3. **Breath and Mantra**: Chant Ek Ong Kaar, Sat Naam, Siree Whaa-hay Guroo in a 2-1/2 breath cycle, in the following manner:

Inhale deeply and as you pull in the navel abruptly, chant *Ek.* Then *Ong Kaar* with an extended sound using all the breath. Give equal time to *Ong* and *Kaar.*

Inhale deeply and as you pull in the navel abruptly, chant *Sat.* Then *Naam* is chanted at the heart center, drawn out until the breath is almost gone. Then, just as you reach the end of the breath, add a quick *Siree* and draw the energy to the brow point.

Inhale half a breath, pull in the navel abruptly, chant *Whaa.* Then *Hay Guroo* as the sound flows up and out of the top of your head. (*Hay* should be relatively short, *Guroo* is drawn out, but not too long.)

The vibration is channeled through the spine, rising from the base to the brow point and beyond. The eyes are closed and focused at the third eye point, and the chin is slightly tucked to create *Jalandhar Bandh* – neck lock - allowing pranic energy to rise smoothly.

Benefits of Chanting Long EkOngKaar

Practicing Morning Call daily opens the heart, clears blockages in the subtle body, and deepens the meditative state. It awakens the dormant creative energy, the kundalini, and connects the practitioner to their higher Self. Many experience a profound inner stillness, a heightened intuition, and a strengthened sense of purpose over time.

Recordings of Long EkOngKaar can be found on the internet, making chanting it a little easier when you are starting out.

There are two ways to find the Divine. One way is to open the solar center, [the 7th chakra, the Sahasrara]. Travel through the naad [of Long Ek Ong Kaar] and charge your solar center and you will get a direct experience of the Divine. The other method is that you concentrate and meditate, and you get this sound in you; thus, it directly charges your crown chakra, and you receive Divine Light...

With one pointedness of the mind, recite [Long Ek Ong Kaar] and that shall be the memory of this day. Open your full heart center and don't feel shy reciting it. It's a call to God, it's a call to the Lord, it is a call to the Divine; let us do it in a humble, honest way. Humble yourself today and pray. Prayer is the power of man. Let us pray, let us pray through these vibrations. – Yogi Bhajan, February 9, 1969

―――――

SOHUNG – THE BREATH OF IDENTITY

Sohung is a sacred sound that has come down through the ages, and it is one of the most timeless mantras to echo from the heart of ancient India. It is not just a word but also a rhythm, woven into the breath of every living being. "So" with the inhale. "Hung" with the exhale. It is the natural music of life itself.

This mantra is often referred to as universal, belonging to no faith or tradition, because it rides on the breath, and every creature breathes. As you chant Sohung in meditation, your breath slows and deepens. Your mind softens. A quiet opens within you, shunya, the stillness of inner space where your concentration expands.

Sohung means "I am That," or "He is me." In a simple but expansive expression, Sohung is an affirmation of oneness with the Divine, "I am. I am." It reminds us that we are not separate from the sacred flow of life. It is a mantra of identity, not ego identity, but essence. It affirms the soul's intimate belonging to something vast and eternal.

Some trace Sohung to the Sanskrit words "so" (that) and "aham" (I am), but many believe its resonance may be even more ancient—perhaps a sound that *preceded* language, the original sigh of consciousness awakening to itself.

In the *Brihadaranyaka Upanishad*, one of the oldest spiritual texts of India, it is said:

> *In the beginning, there was only the Self. Seeing nothing else, the Self declared: 'I am I am.'*

Sohung is this very whisper, still alive in your breath, waiting to be remembered.

How to Chant Sohung

1. **Find a Comfortable Posture**: Sit in a relaxed meditative position. Tilt the chin slightly up in a comfortable and balanced position.

2. **Synchronize Breath with the Chant**: Inhale deeply and chant "So-hung" in a steady, low monotone. Give equal emphasis and duration to the syllables *So*, which is vibrated at the throat and *Hung*, which is vibrated at the forehead. Avoid rushing. Allow the breath to fully release with the chant before inhaling again.

3. **Deepen Your Practice Gradually**: As you continue chanting, it's natural for your rhythm to slow down and your breath to deepen, allowing each cycle to naturally extend in duration.

4. **Begin by chanting for three minutes.** When that is without great effort, gradually extend the time until you are chanting for 11 minutes. If you wish to proceed, please do so. There is no limit to the time you can safely chant Sohung.

When Sohung is chanted, the final sound of "hung" resonates in the throat, with the mouth slightly open and the energy vibrating in the third eye. The back of the tongue is pressed against the back of the throat, and the vibration of that sound penetrates the body like the sound of the conch. This vibration helps focus the consciousness quickly, and you "listen" with your whole being. Sant Baba Gurvinder Singh Mandi explains:

Baba Gurvinder Singh Mandi

The actual bliss of chanting [Sohung in this way] is that the vibration of the entire creation and the universe is in your being. By chanting, you come into a state of sunn samaad   - the bliss of emptiness, where every hair on your body will be chanting this mantra.

MEDITATING ON ONG SOHUNG

My favorite way to experience Sohung is to chant *Ong Sohung*. This mantra acknowledges the presence of the Creative Divine Energy within each being. The components of Ong Sohung can be translated as:

Ong – The creative, omnipotent nature of the Divine.

Sohung – I am that.

Ong Sohung can be chanted aloud from any meditative posture in two breaths, with a quick inhale in between Ong and Sohung. When you have expanded your lung capacity to accommodate it, Ong Sohung is best chanted on a single breath. Guru Singh's recording of Ong Sohung is perfect for meditation and can be found on most streaming services.

- *Ong* is chanted, deeply vibrating the heart center. The sound originates from the throat, with the back of the tongue pressed against the back of the throat, creating a vibration like the sound of a conch being blown. At this spot, the Ida, Pingla, and Sushmana meet, vibrating the pineal and pituitary gland and balancing and stabilizing the nervous system. The lips close as the sound resounds and dissipates.
- *So* is chanted through pursed lips, focusing the energy on the throat chakra.
- *Hung* is again vibrated at the back of the throat, focusing on the forehead, bringing the energy to the third eye point.

Chanting *Ong Sohung* opens the heart center and expands intuition. It cultivates profound self-awareness, affirming that you are both a unique manifestation of material energy and an infinite being of boundless creative potential. The 13th-century Persian Poet Rumi said it beautifully,

You are not a drop in the ocean but the entire ocean in a drop.

KIRTAN KRIYA - SA-TA-NA-MA

Kirtan Kriya is a foundational meditation in the Kundalini Yoga tradition, first taught in the West by Yogi Bhajan. It uses the primal sounds *Sa Ta Na Ma*, which are the *bij*, or seed, forms of the mantra *Sat Naam* —meaning "Truth is my Identity." These syllables represent the cycle of creation: Sa (Infinity), Ta (Life), Na (Death), and Ma (Rebirth).

In this kriya, you chant the mantra aloud, then in a whisper, and then silently. Then, repeat the pattern in reverse, back to chanting aloud. You use a different mudra for each sound and concentrate on visualizing the movement of energy. The combination of sound, rhythm, breath, mudra, and visualization makes Kirtan Kriya a deeply balancing and integrative practice.

This meditation is 30 minutes long, consisting of 5 minutes of chanting aloud, 5 minutes of whispering, 10 minutes of silent chanting, 5 minutes of whispering, and concluding with 5 minutes of chanting aloud. However, you can easily adjust the time to make it shorter or longer, as long as you maintain the ratio of spoken, whispered, and silent chanting. For example, to create a shorter meditation, reduce the chanting and whisper sequence to 1 minute and the silent meditation to 2 minutes, resulting in a total of 6 minutes. That is a good place to start!

The pitch should be a range that is comfortable to you. The sound progression is as follows:

SAA TAA NAA MAA

Pitch and tone of chanting Sa-Ta-Na-Ma.

How to Practice Kirtan Kriya:

1. Sit in a comfortable meditative posture with a straight spine.
2. Chant Sa-Ta-Na-Ma out loud for 5 minutes. As you chant each syllable, press the fingertips to the thumb in this sequence: thumb to index finger on Sa, thumb to middle finger on Ta, thumb to ring finger on Na, and thumb to pinkie finger on Ma.
3. As you chant, visualize a constant inflow of energy into the crown chakra, the Tenth Gate, that moves out of your brow point in an "L" form. For example, as you chant "Sa, the "S" starts at the top of the head, and the "A" moves through your brain and out of your third eye, the Ajna Chakra. Do the same visualization for each syllable. Yogi Bhajan referred to this as the golden cord – the connection between the pineal and pituitary glands.

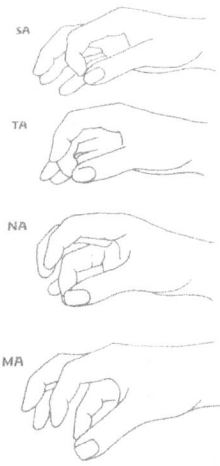

Mudras for Sa-Ta-Na-Ma.

4. After 5 minutes, chant in a whisper for 5 minutes. Continue with the mudra changes and the visualization.
5. After 5 minutes, meditate in silence for 10 minutes. Continue with the mudra changes and the visualization.
6. After 5 minutes, chant in a whisper for 5 minutes. Continue with the mudra changes and the visualization.
7. After 5 minutes, chant out loud for the final 5 minutes. Continue with the mudra changes and the visualization.
8. To end, inhale deeply, exhale and relax for a few minutes.

Benefits of Kirtan Kriya

Kirtan Kriya is renowned for bringing clarity, emotional balance, and deep healing to the mind and nervous system. This meditation enhances mental focus, balances the brain hemispheres, and helps release long-held subconscious patterns. Scientific research supports these claims: a study by Dr. Dharma Singh Khalsa and Dr. Andrew Newberg showed that practicing Kirtan Kriya for just 12 minutes a day over eight weeks significantly improved memory and increased blood flow to areas of the brain associated with cognition and emotional regulation (Khalsa & Newberg, 2015). Another study led by Dr. Helen Lavretsky found that Kirtan Kriya not only reduced depressive symptoms and improved sleep in dementia caregivers but also increased telomerase activity, suggesting measurable benefits for cellular aging and longevity (Lavretsky et al., 2013).

Spiritually, this meditation reconnects you to your true self through the sacred mantra *Sa Ta Na Ma*.

Meditate on this sound. Sa Ta Na Ma, mentally meditate on it and beam it out. Destiny has dignity, dignity has destiny. You are the fortunate ones who will go through this experience. May your Guru and your God stand by you, may the realms of all angels bless you, may the purity of your heart stand by you. May your divine nature help you; may your consciousness get into this, breathe and breathe into the realms of self. – Yogi Bhajan, 12/28/1972

———

GLOSSARY

Amrit Vela – The ambrosial hours, typically the early pre-dawn time considered most conducive for spiritual practice and meditation.

Aquarian Sadhana – A specific early morning practice given by Yogi Bhajan, including Japji Sahib, kriyas, and a sequence of mantras chanted for a set time.

Atma – The eternal Self; the soul or essence of consciousness that underlies one's identity beyond the ego.

Bani – Sacred utterance or spiritual verse; in Sikhism, it refers specifically to the divine hymns revealed by the Gurus and included in the Siri Guru Granth Sahib.

Dasvand – The spiritual discipline of giving 10% of one's income, time, or energy to serve the greater good.

Gyan Mudra – A hand gesture (mudra) in which the tip of the index finger touches the thumb, enhancing receptivity, calmness, and inner awareness.

Jap Sahib – A powerful bani composed by Guru Gobind Singh, recited for strength, courage, and divine protection.

Japji Sahib – The foundational Sikh prayer composed by Guru Nanak, recited as a morning meditation to align with divine wisdom and truth.

Japa – The meditative repetition of a mantra, either silently or aloud, to focus the mind and awaken spiritual energy.

Jalandhar Bandh – Also called neck lock; a yogic technique where the chin is gently tucked toward the chest to straighten the cervical spine and direct energy upward.

Kirtan – Devotional music or chanting that expresses love for the Divine and elevates consciousness through sacred sound.

Kriya – A specific sequence of yogic postures, breathwork, and sound used to produce a desired energetic or spiritual effect.

Laya Yoga – The yoga of absorption through sound, in which the practitioner merges into the rhythm and vibration of mantra or music.

Naam – The sacred Name of the Infinite; divine vibration or consciousness that pervades all.

Naam Simran – The meditative remembrance and repetition of the Divine Name, allowing the sound current to flow through the open heart.

Nadi – Subtle energy channels through which prana flows in the body's energetic system.

Nadi Shodhana – A pranayama practice known as alternate nostril breathing, used to balance energy channels and calm the nervous system.

Prana – The vital lifeforce or energy that animates all living beings; carried through the breath and the subtle body.

Pranayama – Yogic breathing techniques that regulate the flow of prana, harmonize body and mind, and support meditative states.

Sadhak – A spiritual practitioner; one who engages in regular sadhana with dedication and discipline.

Sadhana – A daily spiritual practice undertaken with commitment, discipline, and devotion to self-realization and inner growth.

Sakshi Bhava – The yogic principle of cultivating witness consciousness, observing thoughts and actions without attachment or judgment.

Sankalpa – A heart-centered intention or vow that guides spiritual practice and personal transformation.

Sat Naam – A mantra meaning "Truth is my Identity." It affirms one's connection to the eternal truth within.

Shabad – The sacred sound current; divine vibration expressed through mantra or scripture.

Shabad Guru – The guiding wisdom of the sacred sound; the eternal teacher embodied in the vibration of Divine Truth.

Shakti Pad – A spiritual test phase between disciplined practice and mastery, where the seeker confronts doubt, ego, and identity challenges.

Shavasana – "Corpse pose," a deep relaxation posture practiced at the end of a yoga session to integrate and restore.

Shunya – A state of inner stillness, silence, and emptiness where ego dissolves and pure consciousness is revealed.

Siri Guru Granth Sahib – The sacred scripture of the Sikhs; a compilation of divine revelations by the Sikh Gurus and saints, regarded as the living Guru.

BIBLIOGRAPHY

14 Benefits of Practicing Gratitude (Incl. Journaling). (n.d.). *PositivePsychology.com*. Retrieved from https://positivepsychology.com/benefits-of-gratitude/#:~: text=Gratitude%20strengthens%20relationships%20by%20fostering,more%20posi tive%20outlook%20on%20life.

Benefits of Having a Regular Sadhana Practice. (n.d.). *Bodhi Tree Yoga*. Retrieved from https://bodhitreeyogapai.com/blog/f/benefits-of-having-a-regular-sadhana-practice? blogcategory=niyamas

Brewer, J. A., Worhunsky, P. D., Gray, J. R., Tang, Y. Y., Weber, J., & Kober, H. (2011). Meditation experience is associated with differences in default mode network activity and connectivity. *Proceedings of the National Academy of Sciences, 108*(50), 20254– 20259. https://doi.org/10.1073/pnas.1112029108

Brown, K. W., & Ryan, R. M. (2003). The benefits of being present: Mindfulness and its role in psychological well-being. *Journal of Personality and Social Psychology, 84*(4), 822–848.

Concept of Shunya in Guru Granth Sahib. (n.d.). *Angelfire.com*. Retrieved from https:// www.angelfire.com/realm2/reiki_transcendental/SikhReview/june2000/metaphysic s.htm

Creating a Personalized Meditation Practice: Tips and Strategies. (n.d.). *The Mindfulness App*. Retrieved from https://blog.themindfulnessapp.com/articles/creating-a-person alized-meditation-practice-tips-and-strategies

Datta, A., et al. (2020). Theta and delta EEG activity in meditation and yogic relaxation: A review. *Journal of Clinical Psychology, 76*(5), 950–964.

Divine, M. (2014). *Unbeatable mind: Forge resiliency and mental toughness to succeed at an elite level*. Kokoro Press.

Emmons, R. A., & McCullough, M. E. (2003). Counting blessings versus burdens: An experimental investigation of gratitude and subjective well-being in daily life. *Journal of Personality and Social Psychology, 84*(2), 377–389.

Exploring the Therapeutic Benefits of Pranayama (Yogic Breathing). (n.d.). *PubMed Central*. Retrieved from https://pmc.ncbi.nlm.nih.gov/articles/PMC7336946/

Garrison, K. A., Zeffiro, T. A., Scheinost, D., Constable, R. T., & Brewer, J. A. (2015). Meditation leads to reduced default mode network activity beyond an active task. *Cognitive, Affective, & Behavioral Neuroscience, 15*(3), 712–720.

Goff, P. (2019). *Galileo's error: Foundations for a new science of consciousness*. Pantheon Books.

Goyal, M., Singh, S., Sibinga, E. M., Gould, N. F., Rowland-Seymour, A., Sharma, R., ... & Haythornthwaite, J. A. (2014). Meditation programs for psychological stress and well-being: A systematic review and meta-analysis. *JAMA Internal Medicine, 174*(3), 357–368.

How to Find a Meditation Teacher (6 Key Questions). (n.d.). *Mindworks.org*. Retrieved from https://mindworks.org/blog/how-to-find-a-meditation-teacher/#:~:text=The%20best%20meditation%20instructors%20are,well%2Dliked%20by%20their%20peers.

Iyengar, B. K. S. (1979). *Light on Yoga*. Schocken Books.

Jesus and the Christos: A Gnostic Perspective. (n.d.). *Llewellyn.com*. Retrieved from https://www.llewellyn.com/journal/article/502#:~:text=In%20this%20sense%2C%20Gnostic%20Christianity,a%20state%20of%20Self%2Drealization.

Khalsa, D. S., & Newberg, A. B. (2015). A yoga intervention for cognitive enhancement. *Journal of Alzheimer's Disease, 48*(1), 57–60. https://doi.org/10.3233/JAD-150128

Khalsa, G. S., & Bhajan, Y. (2007). *Sadhana Guidelines: Create Your Daily Spiritual Practice* (3rd ed.). Española, NM: Kundalini Research Institute.

Khalsa, Y. B., & Khalsa, G. S. (2007). *Praana, Praanee, Praanayam: Exploring the breath technology of Kundalini Yoga as taught by Yogi Bhajan*. Kundalini Research Institute.

Kumar, K., et al. (2016). Effect of Yoga Nidra on blood pressure and anxiety. *Indian Journal of Traditional Knowledge, 15*(2), 329–335.

Lama Zopa Rinpoche. (2022). *The Power of Mantra: Vital Practices for Transformation*. Wisdom Publications.

Lavretsky, H., et al. (2013). A pilot study of yogic meditation for family dementia caregivers with depressive symptoms: Effects on mental health, cognition, and telomerase activity. *International Journal of Geriatric Psychiatry, 28*(1), 57–65. https://doi.org/10.1002/gps.3790

Lorenzen, D. N. (1995). Bhakti. In L. Jones (Ed.), *Encyclopedia of Religion* (2nd ed., Vol. 2, pp. 816–821). Macmillan Reference USA.

Mallinson, J., & Singleton, M. (2017). *Roots of Yoga*. Penguin Classics.

Mandair, A.-P. S. (2013). *Religion and the Specter of the West: Sikhism, India, Postcoloniality, and the Politics of Translation*. Columbia University Press.

McCraty, R., Atkinson, M., Tomasino, D., & Bradley, R. T. (2009). The coherent heart: Heart–brain interactions, psychophysiological coherence, and the emergence of system-wide order. *Integral Review, 5*(2), 10–115. https://www.heartmath.org/assets/uploads/2015/01/coherent-heart.pdf

Moszeik, E. N., Stoll, R., & Michalak, J. (2020). The effect of Yoga Nidra and mindfulness on insomnia symptoms and sleep-related stress in a sample with chronic insomnia. *Sleep Science and Practice, 4*(1), 2.

Parker, S. C., et al. (2013). The impact of Yoga Nidra on sleep, anxiety, and well-being in a population of college students. *International Journal of Yoga Therapy, 23*(2), 15–23.

Reflective Practices. (n.d.). *Bakken Center for Spirituality & Healing*. Retrieved from https://csh.umn.edu/academics/whole-systems-healing/reflective-practices

Sahni, P., & Kumar, K. (2018). Effect of Yoga Nidra on heart rate variability and stress in university students. *International Journal of Yoga, 11*(1), 39–45.

Saoji, A. A., Raghavendra, B. R., & Manjunath, N. K. (2019). Effects of yogic breath regulation: A narrative review of scientific evidence. *Journal of Ayurveda and Integrative Medicine, 10*(1), 50–58. https://doi.org/10.1016/j.jaim.2018.08.008

Saraswati, S. S. (1996). *Asana pranayama mudra bandha*. Bihar School of Yoga.

Singh, K. (1989). *Parasaraprasna: Some questions about the Sikhs*. Guru Nanak Dev University.

Singh, N.-G. K. (2005). *The Birth of the Khalsa: A feminist re-memory of Sikh identity*. SUNY Press.

BIBLIOGRAPHY

Singh, P., & Mandair, A.-P. S. (2000). *The Guru Granth Sahib: Canon, meaning and authority*. Oxford University Press.

Sri Guru Granth Sahib. (2004). Translated by Dr. Sant Singh Khalsa. Amritsar: Shiromani Gurdwara Parbandhak Committee. https://www.srigranth.org

Telles, S., et al. (2012). Yogic relaxation through Yoga Nidra decreases blood pressure and increases GSR. *BioPsychoSocial Medicine, 6*, 11.

The Benefits of Sadhana Practice. (n.d.). *Samye Institute*. Retrieved from https://www.samyeinstitute.org/sciences/philosophy/benefits-sadhana-practice/

The Intersection of Technology and Meditation: A New Era of Mindfulness. (n.d.). *How2Shout*. Retrieved from https://news.how2shout.com/the-intersection-of-technology-and-meditation-a-new-era-of-mindfulness/

The Spiritual Teacher and Spiritual Student Relationship. (n.d.). *Spiritual Awakening Process*. Retrieved from https://spiritualawakeningprocess.com/2014/12/the-spiritual-teacher-and-spiritual-student-relationship.html

Vigorous, Calming, Cooling, and Advanced Pranayamas. (n.d.). *Himalayan Institute*. Retrieved from https://himalayaninstitute.org/online/vigorous-calming-cooling-and-advanced-pranayamas/

Yoga Nidra: How It Works and How to Practice It. (n.d.). *Verywell Mind*. Retrieved from https://www.verywellmind.com/yoga-nidra-how-it-works-and-how-to-practice-it-8603941

SHARE YOUR LIGHT: LEAVE A REVIEW

Unlock the Power of Generosity

"The best way to find yourself is to lose yourself in the service of others." – Mahatma Gandhi

Giving without expecting anything in return is one of the most beautiful things we can do. Your kindness can ripple out farther than you know.

Have you enjoyed *The Path of Sadhana*?

Would you like to help someone else, just like you, who is seeking guidance on establishing a daily practice?

Many people choose their next book based on reviews. Your words could help them find a path that brings peace, clarity, and joy.

My mission is to make sadhana simple and inspiring for everyone. But I need your help to reach more hearts.

Leaving a review takes less than a minute—and it's free! But it could truly change someone's spiritual journey.

Your review could help:

1. Someone find their first daily practice.
2. A new seeker feel encouraged to begin.
3. A teacher find words to support others.
4. A small business share sacred teachings.

If this book has touched you in any way, please take a moment to share your thoughts and experiences. You can scan here and go directly to the review page:

https://www.amazon.com/review/review-your-purchases/?asin=B0FBZQPSH1

From my heart to yours—thank you for helping this light reach further.

With gratitude,

Shanti K Khalsa

NOTES

INTRODUCTION

i. The 3HO Foundation stands for *Happy Healthy Holy Foundation*. The 3HO Foundation is a global non-profit organization founded in 1969 by Yogi Bhajan to teach and promote Kundalini Yoga and a lifestyle that supports the integration of body, mind, and spirit.

4. CREATING AND LOVING YOUR OWN SADHANA PRACTICE

i. www.sikhnet.com > files > Banis > Japji - Eng-Rom
ii. https://kundaliniresearchinstitute.org/en/product/peace-lagoon-sacred-songs-of-the-sikhs/
iii. Japji for the Aquarian Age 2.0 is available in English and Spanish and in Apple or Android format.
iv. 3HO.org or Kundaliniresearchinstitute.org

10. MEETING DOUBT AND EMBRACING CHALLENGES

i. KRI International Teacher Training Manual Level 1; The Five Stages on the Path of Wisdom, page 218, Kundalini Research Institute 2020

11. THE SPIRITUAL TEACHER

i. Gautama Buddha. *The Mahāparinirvāṇa Sūtra*. Translated by Kosho Yamamoto, edited by Tony Page. London: Nirvana Publications, 2007.

12. DEEPENING YOUR SADHANA PRACTICE

i. Jugat Guru Singh Khalsa leads several different japa intensives around the world. He is an excellent teacher and holds the collective sanctity of the group with strength and grace. Jugat Guru Singh is also an outstanding mentor on the spiritual path. You can learn more about japa intensives and contact him on Instagram @jugatguru.

www.ingramcontent.com/pod-product-compliance
Lightning Source LLC
Chambersburg PA
CBHW051528120626
46551CB00012B/1125